ENGINEMA

To

With our love for your birthday,

Mum and Dad.

xx

31.3.87

ENGINEMAN S.R.

Michael Jackman

BRADFORD BARTON

ISBN 0 85153 439 2

set and printed by CTP Ltd for Top Link Ltd
for the publishers
D. BRADFORD BARTON LTD
Trethellan House · Truro · England

BD0194

CONTENTS

photographs not otherwise acknowledged are reproduced by permission of Len of Sutton

CHAPTER ONE

Early Days

IT WAS SOON after the commencement of the Autumn Term that I stood before the headmaster of The Roan School at Maze Hill, opposite Greenwich Park and was asked to repeat my request to leave school at Christmas, in order to join the Southern Railway, I was told, in no uncertain terms, that boys who were fortunate enough to be able to attend that ancient school, which opened its doors in the time of Oliver Cromwell, did not leave in order to become engine cleaners! I stood my ground and repeated my request. My parents had already been to see him and said that they did not want me to leave, but would not stand in my way. My grandfather had been a top link driver at Bricklayers Arms, in London's Old Kent Road, and had driven engine No. 240 *Onward*, which had gained a Gold Medal at the Paris Exhibition of 1889. My parents said that I wished to follow in his footsteps.

So it was that a few days before Christmas, 1946, I stood for the last time in the hall of The Roan School and sang 'God dismiss us with thy blessing', a hymn full of meaning for those leaving school, particularly for the only boy in Remove B (the lower fifth form) who was leaving, without the blessing of the school.

My first day at Bricklayers Arms was bitterly cold. The Old Shed had no doors either end and cleaning the tender of 'N' Class 1823 was a chilly experience. The other cleaners laughed when I called the chargeman cleaner 'Sir' – which was a natural thing to do after my years at Roan's. Cleaning engines was the first rung of the ladder of promotion. It was full of practicalities; one learned which pipes were hot, where to hold on and where not to. The senior cleaners called out the parts to be cleaned. The youngest hand (me) did the tender, but by the end of my first day's work I could name fifteen parts of it. On the second day I was allowed to clean the connecting rod of Schools class 928 *Stowe* and whilst busily engaged heard some familiar voices – boys from my form at school had got a shed permit to visit Bricklayers Arms and came over to watch.

The senior cleaner looked at their green blazers with the head of a deer for a badge on the breast pocket and enquired 'Ain't you never seen a Schools before?'. We had a good old chat and the visitors agreed that Jackman was very lucky to be able to touch a Schools. The senior cleaner immediately grinned, gave each of them a wiper, soaked in gas oil, and soon got them to join in when he realised that they were 'my mates'.

Later, he took them up onto the footplate and gave them a demonstration of how to drive, though luckily for all concerned she was 'dead' (no fire in her). They went away overawed by the magic of it all and the thought that Jackman was getting paid Two Pounds and Twopence a week to do this!

On my third day I was told that I was to be messenger since I was, by age, the youngest hand, and the front shift messenger was soon to be promoted to fireman. My cleaning colleagues greeted this decision with cries of 'Lucky devil!' but I retorted that I had joined the Southern to be a cleaner, not a messenger boy. The chargehand replied that I had joined the Southern to be a cleaner and cleaners did as they were told, just as a fireman had to do as his driver told him. That ended the argument. . . .

Each locomotive depot had two messengers – a front shift and a back shift. One worked from 7 a.m. to 3 p.m. one week and then 2 p.m. to 10 p.m. the next, the same as the cleaners under 16 years old. Cleaners over 16 did a night shift, 10 p.m. to 6 a.m. So on the Thursday I travelled about with Regan, the 'retiring' messenger. Up to Waterloo station at 7 a.m., walking to London Bridge (time allowed, 35 minutes), pick up internal mail for Bricklayers Arms there in the special room provided, on the train to Waterloo Eastern, into the Messenger room, collect more mail, then onto the Stores Offices in Addington Street (after a cup of tea and a bun in the Waterloo Staff Canteen) and onto a 53A bus back to the depot, arriving at 8.50. Officially the Messenger had to clean the Breakdown Crane when not engaged in running about, of which there was plenty, but spare parts for engines waiting for repair kept the messenger busy. Over to Stewarts Lane for bits for a King Arthur, meet a train from Eastleigh to collect parts for a West Country. Every morning on the tram to New Cross Gate loco to collect the enginemen's time sheets, to be brought back to Bricklayers Arms for the Accounts Section. The crane, I must say, got very little cleaning. On the back shift; an afternoon visit to New Cross Gate, back to the depot, then round the offices to collect mail for Waterloo and all depots on the Southern, then down to the LEDSO (London East Divisional Superintendent's Office) at Orpington to collect general and special locomotive workings which were prepared there.

I was given a Railway Service Badge to wear, although these badges were intended for use in the Second World War only. They allowed the wearer access to restricted places, including in my case, a front-row view when our Queen and Prince Philip left Waterloo Station en route to Romsey for the first part of their honeymoon.

Since the job involved a lot of rail travel, I had permanent possession of a Motorman's Cab Pass to enable me to show ticket collectors. I was told that the holding of this pass did not allow me to ride in the motorman's cab. Regan, however, informed me that most 'juice blokes' (electric train drivers) did not object as long as you asked them properly and I had many an interesting cab trip down to Orpington and back. The railway mail system enabled a Stores Clerk at say Ramsgate to write to his opposite number at Bournemouth depot in order to borrow parts needed to get an engine back in service. The messenger system saw to it that mail took no more than 24 hours to reach any part of the Southern system.

The days flew by and I had visited most depots in the London Area by the time I was showing another lad the duties before preparing to become a fireman. Training for the footplate was done by spending time with the firelighters – seeing how an engine was 'lit up' and the fire built up over a period of twelve hours, allowing every part of the engine to gradually warm through. All too often in practice, fire was taken from one engine and placed in 'dead' engines' fireboxes with no time for warming through. Time was also spent with the boilermakers, going inside fireboxes which, though empty of fire, were still very warm indeed and with a high pressure of steam still in the boiler. The fitters showed how engines were repaired, how the notes a driver made on his repair card were of help (and sometime a hindrance) to the fitter's diagnosis of its faults. A favourite task given by fitters to trainee firemen was to get them to undo the mass of screws which held the air-smoothed casing on the West Country and Battle of Britain class Pacifics – the 'Spam Cans'. Unblocking the sanding gear of the Spams was another little chore given to the fitters' temporary assistants. Bricklayers Arms at that time had a few women labourers who greased tender axleboxes, since the engine crew were only responsible for above the tender wheels – i.e. coal and water. It was the responsibility of the fitting staff to see that tender axleboxes were fully greased, the engine crew being entirely responsible for the locomotive. The only exception to this rule was the oil bath on the Pacifics, for which only the fitting staff were responsible.

In those early years after the war, the railways had many EVW's (European Voluntary Workers), many of whom were from Poland. Bricklayers Arms had quite a few and many of them lived in an L.C.C. school on the corner of Marlborough Grove and Rolls Road, close to the Bricklayers Arms branch line. Most of them were a cheery lot and eagerly taught Polish to anyone who would help them with their English. The Poles worked with the fitting staff, many as labourers and were taught Cockney dialect, complete with all the swear words. They in turn, taught the fitters Polish swear words, and all in all the system worked well. The Polish names which, like Welsh, seemed to have little need of vowels – for many consisted solely of a string of consonants – led to a rather amusing incident when I and several other cleaners from Bricklayers Arms went up to the Railway Doctor at London Bridge to pass the stiff medical and even harder eyesight test before being passed as firemen. After the colour tests, came the sight reading card. The lad in front of me was asked to read the bottom line which was something like 'Z Y C L N S C W K'. There was utter silence from the lad. 'Come along, come along – can't you see it?' asked the doctor, with some impatience. 'See it, guv'ner? Blimey, me sister goes out with him!' came the reply.

A short time later came a trip on the footplate as third man, down to Paddock Wood via Maidstone. On returning to the depot, Inspector Mockeridge asked me a few questions on rules, hand signals and fixed signals and I was pronounced fit for footplate duties.

CHAPTER TWO

First Firing Turns

THE FIRST ENGINE I officially fired on was No. 2463, an ex-L.B.S.C. E4 tank, on my sixteenth birthday. The location was Willow Walk Yard. I'll not forget that first duty. It was pouring with rain and after signing on at 11 p.m., I walked with Driver Miller, an ex-Brighton man who had migrated from New Cross to Bricklayers Arms, to relieve the men who had signed on at 3.20 that afternoon. Driver Miller was not impressed with the standard of Bricklayers Arms firemen he had come into contact with since coming there. New Cross had ceased to be a depot in its own right and from 1947 had become surplus to requirements, due to the reorganisation of motive power depots, hence the unwilling influx of New Cross men. Driver Miller was still unimpressed with the standard of our firemen after my 9½ hours with him! He told me that I could not fire to my mother's kitchen boiler, which was probably near the truth.

Finishing my first turn of duty at 8.30 Sunday morning, I looked on the Alteration Sheet to find that I was booked to be on duty at 9.50 Monday morning, and against my name was the notation 'Pass. to New Cross Gate'. Here I made the acquaintance of Driver Harry Hemsley and during the morning he showed me how to fire to an E5 Radial while we shunted up and down at Goodwood Road and down to Ballarat Siding. By the mid-afternoon I had got hold of the idea and had begun to feel that Driver Miller's pronunciation was unfounded.

However, at 5 p.m. we went over to the sidings known as 'The Field' and hooked on to nine coaches to take up to London Bridge, to form the 5.40 to Tunbridge Wells via Oxted. Hemsley told me to make up the fire and get the boiler full. All too soon, the road was set and it was 'right away' to London Bridge – we made it, just! Driver Hemsley shook his head upon arrival at London Bridge. The water was in the bottom nut of the gauge glass and we had about 120 lbs of steam, which just about kept the vacuum brake off as we struggled into the terminus. By six o'clock we were back at New Cross loco, where I had to clean the fire and empty the smokebox and ashpan. This procedure was known as 'putting her away', then she had to be 'got ready' which, for my part, consisted of filling the sand boxes, trimming and re-filling the paraffin headlamps, making up the fire and trimming the coal on the bunker and finally filling the tanks with water. By the time all this was over it was 7.30 and I had half an hour to get back to Bricklayers Arms and sign off at 8 p.m. I had this duty for the rest of the week, by which time Driver Hemsley had taught me a lot. Sunday I was on duty at 6 a.m. 'As Required', which meant putting engines away and getting them ready. As a very junior fireman, I was not booked with a regular driver and upon looking at my next turn of duty for the Monday, I found I was 9 p.m. 'Pass. to New Cross Gate', with an added notation 'Shed Pilot'.

Having worked the previous week around New Cross, I could not help wondering what I would be doing there since during the day the Loco. Depot there only seemed to be used by visiting engines from Tunbridge Wells West and Brighton, to turn round and get ready in order to run light up to London Bridge. The night stud of engines numbered four and the job of the shed engineman there (with my assistance) was to ensure that the engines had sufficient water in the boiler and a decent bit of fire in them. By midnight we had seen to our charges and slept until half-past three, when the noise of the Brighton paper train woke me up (but not the driver) and I made a tour of inspection of our engines, then finding all was well, resumed my broken sleep. At six a.m. it was back on the tram to Bricklayers Arms and sign off at 6.30. I learned very little that week. By Thursday, I was staying up all through the day, going to the cinema before going on duty and during the morning spending time working on my outdoor O gauge model railway.

On the Friday night I arrived at Bricklayers Arms, ready for a night's sleep. As I signed on, Jim Foote, the foreman, put his arm on my shoulder.

'How long have you been firing?' he enquired.
'Two weeks', I replied, quite proudly.
'Right', he said. 'You are senior to young Martin sitting in the enginemen's lobby. He will do your turn at The Gate; you can go out onto Four Road, Old Shed, and help Percy Garrish get 1823 ready!' I walked over to 1823 and could not stifle a yawn. Percy Garrish was another ex-New Cross driver and welcomed me with a thin smile. 'I hope you are better than the bloke I had last night', he said. 'We came to a stand at Forest Hill – SOS'. Those dreaded initials on a driver's ticket indicated 'Short of Steam'.

It then dawned on me, I was to be fireman on a night goods down the Brighton main line and the last sleep I had had was at 5.30 that morning! I scrambled up onto the tender and started to break up the large lumps of coal. Garrish looked at me. 'Before you break them all up, how about filling up the firebox first? We ain't got much in there!' I saw a look of disbelief in his eyes as he went on, 'Old Footie said you were an experienced fireman! How long you been at it? You haven't got an S.R. cap badge?' (After doing 313 firing turns a fireman gained his 'S.R. ENGINEMAN' cap badge, an indication of his length of service on the shovel). I swallowed as I told him that this was the end of my second week. . . .

Poor old Percy stopped what he was doing and shook his head; 'Oh, my good Gawd!' was all he said. By 10 we had left the Loco and went down to Willow Walk, where only two weeks before I had helped make up trains. We backed onto a line of wagons that curved away into the distance and I heard the guard say to my driver, 'Seventy five and a brake, mate! Hope you've got a decent stoker up there tonight. I missed my break time at Three Bridges last night as you were so late!' I learned later that guards always referred to drivers losing time, but if one made up time it was always referred to as being the guard's doing. My driver's reply was double-edged. 'Oh my fireman's all right! He's been at it for two whole weeks!' I could not hear the guard's reply; perhaps it was just as well.

We had a banker from Willow Walk all the way to Forest Hill and we needed her. Passing my home station of Forest Hill, we had 150 lbs 'on the clock', instead of the desired 200 and not too much water in the boiler. The welcome slight descent through Sydenham and Penge helped the boiler to recover and Percy took over the shovel for a few minutes. 'Keep her full up in the back corners and under the door', he advised. I did my best and got the pressure up to 190 as we passed

Norwood Junction. Percy then opened her out and I should imagine the cut-off was around 40 per cent approaching East Croydon. He pointed to the fire-hole door. 'She needs feeding again! Come on now!' Sweat was trickling down my face and neck. I finished a round of firing and put the injector on again. His hand pointed to the fire-hole door. 'Come on', he said. Again, another seven shovelfuls into the glaring fire, then using the short rake, pulled more coal forward into the hole above the shovel plate.

From East Croydon the line rises steadily at 1 in 264 to Coulsdon North, steepening to a final two mile stretch at 1 in 164 up to the entrance to Quarry Tunnel. Driver Garrish was hurrying the long train of loose-coupled wagons, keeping the couplings taut to avoid a snatch as the gradient steepened. Through Coulsdon North station we went, sparks flying from the chimney of No. 1823: another round of coal; 190 on the clock; Garrish increased the cut-off and how she barked up that next couple of miles. Then ahead was the entrance to Quarry Tunnel; the regulator was eased slightly and down into the tunnel we plunged. Half a boiler full of water and almost 200 lbs of steam. Percy left his side of the footplate and came over to me and shouted in my ear, 'Let the fire burn through, then two more rounds – one through Earlswood and another through Horley and that will do her. We come off at Three Bridges and she stands there for five minutes – no use blowing her head off'. I nodded and took the opportunity of spraying the tender with water to keep down the dust. Just before Horley, the regulator was opened out and took us quickly up the last 4½ miles to Three Bridges, where we drew to a gentle stop. Three Bridges men relieved us and we walked over to the small shed there, where we ate our sandwiches. I suddenly realised how tired I was and asked what our next duty was. 'We relieve in the station and bring the fast goods back to Willow Walk', came the reply. I closed my eyes, promising myself never to neglect my sleep again, no matter what.

Half hour later, feeling very tired, we climbed onto the footplate of a Brighton K class Mogul, the number of which I cannot remember. The fire was beautifully made up and Percy Garrish looked at it and told me to sit down. 'It's roughly five miles down at 1 in 264 to Horley then about the same distance uphill to the exit of Quarry Tunnel, then downhill all the way home. So all you have to do is set the Weir pump at a slow rate so as not to knock her back for steam'.

The Weir pump forced cold water into the boiler whereas the injector forced hot water, so that Brighton drivers tended to see that the Weir pump was only used when an engine had little hard work to do. It was a splendid run back and I was impressed with the smooth riding of the Brighton Mogul as opposed to the slight jerky movement of the South Eastern one. Once into our home loco it was the usual put-away and get ready and I finished duty around 7 a.m. Needless to say I went home and straight to bed.

Just as well, because when I booked on night at 9 p.m., Foreman Foote was waiting for me. 'Ah', he said. 'Old Percy Garrish wants you again tonight – his regular mate is still off sick – 1823 on Four Road.' I had an even better run up Forest Hill bank and even got her blowing off through Sydenham. Percy grinned, 'Amazing what a good night's sleep can do', he said. Coming back, the Brighton Mogul had not got such a good fire as on the previous trip and I found how hard it was to master the tip-flap firehole door on them, especially when it came to filling up the back corners of the firebox. Nevertheless, Percy showed me how to twist the shovel when it was well inside the door, but it was nowhere near as easy as firing an 'N' class.

My third week of firing was again done at New Cross. Signing on at 11.55 a.m. it was pass to New Cross Gate and there I met the imposing figure of Driver Winifrith – a handle-bar moustache, highly polished London, Brighton & South Coast cap badge, spotless overalls and boots you could literally see your face in. He reminded me of some photographs I had seen of Brighton enginemen of fifty years before. He merely nodded when I said, 'Good afternoon! I'm Fireman Jackman from Bricklayers Arms. I was told I was to be your mate'. He then consulted his watch and after waiting another three or four minutes in silence got up and beckoned me to follow him. We walked through the sidings and relieved on a E5 Radial. He told me what trains we would be making up and that he wanted no smoke, no blowing off steam and he expected me to service the Westinghouse donkey pump when we stopped for a cup of tea at 4 p.m. I hadn't a clue how to do this, but he soon showed me, once – but it was a clear demonstration of how to look after this important piece of Brighton engine equipment, and was to be invaluable in the years ahead.

Driver Winifrith did not engage in chat, and the next three days passed slowly. Each day we used to watch the 4.20 from London Bridge to Brighton via Sheffield Park thunder through, a Brighton Atlantic on the front, her whistle blowing as she swept past New Cross Loco, with ex-New Cross men – now reluctantly Bricklayers Arms based, but still 100 per cent New Cross men – in charge. On the third day, I ventured to enquire, 'What's her first stop?' 'Croydon East', came the reply, 'AND they have to pass Forest Hill in nine minutes'. It was to be some years before I had the 4.20, and with nine on and a 'Midland' tank, passing Forest Hill in nine took some doing. In my early innocence I imagined the nine minutes to be from passing New Cross Gate to passing Forest Hill, but later found out the nine minutes allowed was from leaving London Bridge!

On the Thursday I mentioned that my grandfather had driven 240 *Onward* and that engine had gone faster than the competitive Brighton engine No. 189 *Edwin Blount* in the trials on the French P.L.M. railway in 1889. Driver Winifrith nodded and then went on to describe the engines he had fired on and how the fireboxes of the Atlantics would be filled up at Victoria and take them all the way to Brighton.

The next few weeks were spent in the yard at Bricklayers Arms, getting engines ready, putting them away; then I was put into the No. 9 link, shunting all over the Bricklayers Arms branch line – High Level, No. 3 Yard, Willow Walk, Sorting Sidings and at Rotherhithe Road carriage sidings. Sometimes my driver was a newly Passed Fireman and it was not long before one of them said, 'Come over this side and see how we do it'. Under careful tuition, I started to handle the regulator and the quick-acting Westinghouse Air brake. Soon, we split the shift in half, each taking turns to be driver and fireman. It was exacting work and needed close concentration, being not half as easy as it looked. The shunters worked hard, running alongside, unhooking, holding their shunting poles under one arm like a gamekeeper carries a gun and waving their four-aspect hand-lamps, changing them from white to green (for slow down) to red (for stop) by a quick flick of the wrist. I tried to do it one day, missed the coupling, dropped the shunting pole (which my engine ran over) and tripped on some signal wires, tearing my jacket. I returned to the footplate defeated!

Various drivers, in the quiet periods between making up trains, began explaining the Rule Book to me. Drivers recalled how they used to fire to various types of locomotives and generally their advice agreed with each other, so that I acquired a good idea how to handle the wide variety of engines that one had to work on. Firing had to be 'tuned' to the driving method employed, however, as will be seen in the following chapters.

Bricklayers Arms motive power depot consisted, at this period, of some 125 locomotives made up of 49 ex-S.E.C.R. types – four 'N' class 2–6–0; six 'E1' rebuilds 4–4–0; seven 'E' 4–4–0; four 'D' 4–4–0;

twelve ‘C’ 0–6–0; four ‘01’ 0–6–0; eleven ‘H’ 0–4–4T; and one ‘S’ 0–6–0 saddle tank. The Southern Railway types were – four King Arthur 4–6–0; sixteen Schools 4–4–0; ten ‘L1’ 4–4–0; and two ‘UI’ 2—6—0; totalling 32. And finally 40 ex-L.B.S.C.R locomotives – three ‘11X’ 4–4–2T; three ‘B4X’ 4–4–0; two ‘E1’ 0–6–0T; ten ‘E3’ 0–6–2T; eight ‘E4’ 0–6–2T: three ‘E5’ 0–6–2T; five ‘E6’ 0–6–2T; and six ‘C2X’ 0–6–0. The last but by no means least in the stud were four of the big 2–8–0 W.D Austerity engines.

Daily visitors to the depot were Battle of Britain and West Country class Pacifics, together with ‘Q’ class 0–6–0s from Tunbridge Wells, ‘J’ class 4–6–2Ts (also from The Wells), ‘H1’ and ‘H 2 Atlantics from Newhaven, ‘Q1’ Charlies from Tonbridge, and 13 tanks from Brighton and Tunbridge Wells. One was expected to be able to fire to any of these types – and frequently did so!

Bricklayers Arms opened in 1844, when the South Eastern and London & Croydon Railways built the branch line to their independent London terminus at Bricklayers Arms station, in order to avoid paying the high toll charges imposed by the London & Greenwich Railway for using their tracks into and out of London Bridge. The opening of the branch forced the Greenwich company to reduce its tolls and this finished Bricklayers Arms as a passenger station for regular services. The loco shed and the branch line remained, however, and concentrated on goods traffic. Originally the South Eastern had used New Cross locomotive sheds, opened by the London & Croydon Railway in 1838, but transferred all its locomotives to Bricklayers Arms in 1845, Croydon engines reverting to New Cross. One hundred and twelve years later, Bricklayers Arms became the new home for engines from the depot which had been ‘home’ for South Eastern engines. Willow Walk sidings were given to the London Brighton & South Coast Railway in exchange for free running powers over the L.B.S.C.R. metals between Corbetts Lane and Norwood Junction, so that ‘Brighton’ engines were regularly seen on the Bricklayers Arms branch from 1849 onward. Locomotives from Bricklayers Arms travelling to London Bridge, and later Cannon Street and Charing Cross, had to run onto the main line and reverse at North Kent East. Carriage stock from Rotherhithe Road sidings, of course, had to use the same procedure, causing the Rotherhithe Road pilot engine to have to draw empty trains for London out onto the main line with a train engine attached to the London end, necessitating uncoupling on the main line – a procedure which caused delays. In later years much of the main line stock was berthed on the lines between Metropolitan Junction and Charing Cross (on the up and down middle roads). Later on, stock was taken to Stewarts Lane in the morning or to Blackheath and Grove Park and returned in the mid afternoon in time for the evening 'rush hours'.

The loco depot itself consisted of three sheds. First was the Old Shed, opened in 1844 and part of the original engine house, but in 1947 consisting of eight roads. The next shed was the Carriage Shed, consisting of four roads, which used to hold carriages until Rotherhithe Road was opened in 1870. This shed had the alternative name of 'St. Patricks' since legend had it that the Carriage Department moved out to Rotherhithe Road and handed the shed over to the Loco Department on March 17th 1870, though no official records remain to confirm this supposition. The 'New' Shed was opened in 1870.

The Running Foreman's office faced the outgoing and incoming tracks, with the coal stage on his right – so he could see all that went on there, too! A long corridor ran from the foreman's dusty, smoky office, behind which were the telephone attendant-come-clerk, the list clerk, who made out the duty rosters and the alteration sheet, the Running Superintendent, whom one saw when late for duty. On the walls opposite these little open offices were the Engineman's Daily Notices (Speed Restrictions, No water at . . ., etc.), Duty Rosters, Holiday lists, daily Alteration Sheet and Union notices. In the window of the telephone attendant's office were notes left by one engineman for another, which were the only means of communication between men since, although they might be in the same link, they rarely met. Many of the notes were requests to change duties but mainly to ensure that the relieving crew looked at the Alteration Sheet and advise the crew they were relieving if their turn of duty had been altered, thereby saving a trip back from London Bridge to Bricklayers Arms – highly irregular, but always carried out!

Enginemen worked in a twelve week rota and prior to mid 1948, worked a thirteen day fortnight – for example one could be back shift Sunday starting at say 10 p.m., finishing the week on Saturday night by signing on at 11.55 p.m., finishing say 9 a.m. Sunday morning with the rest of Sunday off but being booked to sign on at 12.5 a.m. (Five past midnight) Monday morning, finishing the week by a 4 a.m. Saturday morning duty finishing mid-day, then be booked for Sunday afternoon duty at 2 p.m. and so on. With the introduction of Rest Days in the middle of a week or indeed any day, there were insufficient men to enable the days to be taken off, so that we had to work them, even though the duty was 'covered' by another pair of men. So, as an example of this complicated piece of union achievement, which was much needed, No. 1 link Rest Day working was covered by No. 3 link men; No. 2 link was covered by No. 4 link, both of which had 'spare' duties available. In the Summer periods, the senior links covered their own rest day workings, whilst Nos. 3 and 4 got the Summer Specials, more of which a little later on.

In the early March I went into No. 6 link, which covered No. 4 duties. Enginemen's holidays were spread between March and October, and they were lucky to get one real summer vacation more than once in five years, since that was the busiest time. My driver was Jack Glew, an Improvement Class Instructor and my last mate had suggested to me that I had my Rule Book with me at all times when working with 'Mr. Glew'. Jack Glew wore a check golfing cap and was always a very smartly turned-out driver. He had had the misfortune to fall off the tender of an engine as a fireman and had sustained back injuries which precluded him for working any engine with a stick-lever reversing gear. As a 'compensationary case', agreed by the company doctor, this meant that Jack could not work in the shunting yards other than with an 'H' Class tank which had steam reverse. Since Rotherhithe Road was the 'H' class venue and was covered solely by ex-main line drivers in what was disparagingly called by firemen 'The Old Man's Gang', Jack did little of the shunting duties – which used to annoy certain members of his link, not that that bothered Jack. So I was fortunate in being his fireman, though I did not realise it at first.

Our first duty together was to take a Schools down to Rotherhithe Road, then empties to Cannon Street and prepare the engine for the dreaded 6.18 down to Dover. Jack helped me get down half a ton of large knobs of coal and these were carefully distributed into the back corners and under the door of the firebox. Jack saw to it that every decent bit of coal was shovelled forward and piled up in a safe pyramid, the tip of which was central to the shovel plate, ensuring that the main line fireman had plenty of coal – and good coal at that, for his journey down. Cab lights (windows) were cleaned inside and out while Jack carefully oiled up. The footplate was washed down with the spray pipe and he saw to it that I tightened the smokebox door before putting on the headlamps, freshly cleaned, filled and trimmed by me. Although we stood on Cannon Street Bridge for nearly two hours, I was not still for more than a minute before he would ask had I checked this or that. . . .

About 5.30 he suggested I had a wash in the tool bucket (the usual washing facility for enginemen) and then sat down. I did the same. 'Do you carry your Rule Book?' he enquired. I took it out of my serge jacket hanging in the clothes cupboard. He smiled. 'Good! Do you read it?'

'Yes', I answered, adding 'It's a bit complicated'.

'You read but obviously don't analyse it!' he answered.

He proceeded to analyse the sets of rules without the necessity to look at the Book, by dividing them into groups – Rules 1–16, Discipline; 34–49 Various fixed signals; 50–54 Hand signals; and so on. It made a lot more sense the way he explained it.

'What does a green light mean?' he suddenly enquired.

Without thinking, I said the obvious, 'Clear to go.'

'Oh, really? What about the shunter's green hand signal?'

'Ah! That means slow down.'

'And what about a signalman waving a green light from side to side as you pass his box?'

I shook my head. 'Don't know.'

'It means, sonny, that your bloody train is divided!'

He then enumerated the various meanings of a green light. He explained that white was the original 'all clear' signal, that green on a distant indicated it was off and red was at caution, yellow not being substituted until the turn of the century. He impressed upon me that a green handsignal's meaning depends on who was giving it and where. Thereafter I read my Rule Book at a slower pace and with much more interest. . . .

By 6 p.m. Jack had made a brake, which the guard destroyed as test. I put on my jacket as the wind was cold, and looked down the platform for the No. 2 link men due to come and relieve us. Jack pushed some burnt-through coal down the front end of the box and put seven shovelfuls over the front. He then put the blower on, just a touch, so as not to cover the signalbox in smoke. At ten-past six the guard came up and wanted to take Jack's name. Jack said that we should be relieved at any minute, but the guard insisted; he then informed him that we had ten on and walked back down the train. Jack took a copy of the Working Timetable from his jacket and read out, 'Sevenoaks, Tonbridge and Ashford'.

I had heard about the 6.18 and the complaints about its late running. Back in those days, few people had cars and relied upon buses connecting at their nearest station to take them home. If the train was a few minutes late, the buses left in order to make other connections on their journey, leaving some very angry season ticket holders, who then wrote to Waterloo. The un-social hours worked by railwaymen did not encourage recruits and the result was any absenteeism or sickness (which was without pay!) meant that unskilled firemen had to stand in, which often resulted in SOS being entered on the Lost Time Ticket, which was issued by the train guard for any loss in excess of one minute. My thoughts on this were interrupted by Driver Glew.

'Ever been to Ashford in a hurry, Mike?'

'No, Jack! But I expect I am about to!'

Off with the serge jacket, which went back into the clothes cupboard. Switch on the hydrostatic lubricator, already set at the usual three drops a minute; damper wide open; boiler full; steam pressure hovering on 220; Schools class 923 *Bradfield* was ready to go. A blast from the guard's whistle; a green hand signal held steadily above his head; two yellow aspects on the starting signal as Jack sounded the whistle and opened the regulator fully into the first port, then eased it slightly. 923 moved easily away. We were off!

With a sharp staccato bark, the Schools attacked the sharp left hand curve out of Cannon Street, Jack leaning well out to get a good look at the signals at Borough Market Junction. 'Green!' he shouted and his hand pointed to the firehole door. Seven shovelfuls placed to the very best of my ability – one to each front corner, one half way down each side, one into each back corner plus one under the door. He pointed to the injector. On it went. Round to the right curved the track on the approach to London Bridge. I saw the signal. 'Green down 3'. I called out. Jack nodded and increased the cut-off slightly, pointing to the firehole door again. Seven more into the box. I looked anxiously at the steam pressure gauge – 215, and went to shut off the injector. 'Leave it on – you have got to fight it all the way to Knockholt. Watch the chimney. When the smoke is almost clear, fire again without me having to tell you!' Those two short sentences were excellent advice and I dutifully watched the chimney as well as the road ahead. Sure enough, as soon as the smoke thinned, another seven shovelfuls held her on 215. Over the arches, past Peak Freans, another seven. I looked down at the entrance to the Bricklayers Arms branch and saw an 'H' class tank with one of my ex-cleaner colleagues gaping up at me. I waved to him, and he waved back, after a fashion. 'How fast?' I shouted.

Jack answered, 'About 55 – Fire now, then keep the doors shut until we pass through New Cross Station and Tanners Hill Tunnel, otherwise you might get a blow-back due to the low clearances.' I finished firing as we swept through New Cross and saw Jack give the blower a half-turn to keep the fire inside the firebox as we passed under New Cross Road bridge and then swiftly through Tanners Hill Tunnel. He shouted again, 'Fire now, then you won't be thrown across the footplate when we make the right hand curve past St. Johns.' I just about finished firing and caught a glimpse of St. Johns starter at green and held out my left hand. 'Green,' I shouted and 923 took the right hand curve sharply. Jack tested the water gauge glass on his side. 'Shut off the injector, but don't let her blow-off.' I shut it off and watched the pressure gauge creep from 215 to 220, then on with the injector. I fired again; Hither Green. The climb had steepened to 1 in 140 for 1½ miles, then it got worse to 1 in 120 for another 2¼ miles to Elmstead Woods. On the adjacent track was the 6.16 Cannon Street to Ramsgate, via Chatham, with a Spam on the front, pulling slowly away from us. I found out later that with the usual No. 2 link men on the 6.18, they used to try and race the 6.16 to Chislehurst but no doubt Jack in his wisdom decided not to extend 923 and her fireman of barely three months' experience. . . .

Jack took the shovel from me and, using it as a shield, looked into the shaking, molten fire, quivering like a white-hot jelly under the door. 'Get a bit more over the front, but otherwise it's not too bad,' he advised before resuming his vigil leaning out of the cab, looking into the darkness ahead. I set to and kept up a steady firing rate. I was glad that Jack had made me throw forward all of the best coal; there was now a sizeable 'hole' made in the pyramid I had shovelled forward.

Approaching Orpington, Jack shouted, 'Sound the whistle long and hard and wake those b———s up in the Control Office as we go through!' I did this with pleasure, remembering the hours I had had to wait as a messenger while the new engine workings were printed.

Chelsfield – another 2 miles of 1 in 120, then half a mile at 1 in 170 to the summit just past Knockholt. Speed was in the low forties now as *Bradfield* finished the gruelling 11¾ mile climb from New Cross. I fired again, then Jack pointed ahead. 'There! Isn't that a lovely sight? Bridge 179. The bridge of sighs and you still have 210 on the clock. We'll make a fireman of you yet!' Jack told me to make up the fire then half close the dampers since it was nearly four miles down at 1 in 145 through Polhill Tunnel and Dunton Green. The impetus took the train easily up the 1 in 160 gradient to Sevenoaks, where we made our first stop. All this time, Jack had not looked at his watch once, but as we came to a halt in Sevenoaks station he glanced at it under the station lights. 'Half-a-minute down,' he commented. Damper opened wide. Injector off. Boiler pressure 215 and rising fast. 'It's uphill to the mouth of Sevenoaks Tunnel then downhill all the way to Tonbridge. Rake the coal forward in the tender and give it a good dampening down. Keep your fire well up because after the Tonbridge stop – where we want to stop right for water – we start to get a move on.'

I nodded and hoped I could stop the engine right for water, since the water crane was on my side. But I need not have bothered. Jack had made a half brake application and put the handle back into the running position while I was trying to judge where to shout 'Stop!'

We topped up the tender with about a thousand gallons of water and at 7.4 p.m. left Tonbridge, dead on time for the 26½-mile dash to Ashford, where we were due in at 7.35 – an average start to stop of 51 m.p.h. The almost dead-straight line of this run was ideal for regaining time and engines on a non-stop through Tonbridge have been known to have passed Ashford in a few seconds over 19½ minutes – an average speed of over 81 m.p.h.! However, our progress to Ashford was not as spectacular as this, but suffice to say we arrived at 7.34.

The return half of this duty was the 9.40 to Holborn Viaduct via Maidstone East, but Ashford loco provided their own men to cover this, so we rode home 'on the cushions', since we were due to finish duty at 9.30 and were late enough as it was! That first real taste of main line running is as clear today as if it were only yeterday.

CHAPTER THREE

Moving up

WITH THE START of the racing season, the Southern used to put on many special trains for race-goers. One morning Driver Glew and I signed on at the gentlemanly hour of 8.45 a.m., walked up to London Bridge and relieved on an up Dover train. After running into Cannon Street, we took the engine to Ewer Street for coal and water and to clean the fire, for with this engine we were to run the 11.05 from Charing Cross, call at Waterloo then fast to Westenhanger. Whilst cleaning the fire, I noticed that the fire at the front end of the box was black-out. A close look revealed a leaking tube; Jack took one look and said that we should need another steed – which was a pity since the engine 924 *Haileybury* would have been a fine one for the nine coaches that were diagrammed for this Race Train.

Jack rang Bricklayers Arms, who said another engine would be sent and we were to proceed to Charing Cross where the exchange would be made. The time was just ten o'clock. We ran light to 'The Cross' and were stood out on the bridge. 10.30 came and no sign of another engine. We had made the fire up, partly to keep the front end warm and partly to run the train out on time and perhaps exchange engines at Tonbridge, which would have entailed a special stop and delay. At five to eleven, smoke in the direction of Waterloo East; yes, a light engine was approaching, not a School – that was too much to hope for – but an 'L1', No. 1757. With little time to spare, she was signalled back onto the well-filled train. I left *Haileybury*, walked carefully over the bridge and relieved the Bricklayers Arms fireman on 1757, who had managed to build a good fire in the short time available. Driver Woodbridge left 1757 and relieved Jack Glew (engines were never allowed to be unmanned not even for a few minutes, when on a running road). Jack had a look at the fire and commented, 'Keep it like that'. 11.05 came the Right Away, first stop Waterloo (East) then next stop Westenhanger. The loud bark of the 'L1' sounded as if the engine was being worked harder than it actually was and Jack shouted over 'Don't listen to her bark; watch the chimney!'

Some firemen preferred a flat fire on an L1 but 1757 had a deeper one, with the back corners and under the door built up to the height of the firehole door mouthpiece. So I kept it that way and she held on to her full working pressure of 180 until we got to Grove Park where, as the gradient stiffened, she began to drop back to 160. Driver Glew had a look at the fire and smiled. 'You are working too hard! Let the fire burn through – I'll tell you when'.

Elmstead Woods came and went, and still no word from Jack. Approaching Chislehurst, he pointed to the firehole doors. 'Seven', he shouted and handed the doors for me. The injector was off and pressure had risen to 175, with half a glass of water showing with the regulator fully open in the first port. The fire was almost too bright to look at and I slowed down my rate of firing and soon the injector was on and 1757 was back on 180. An 'L1' needed careful firing and the tendency to overfire due to their deep throated exhaust was the usual cause of poor steaming for the majority of the class. Jack eased the regulator approaching Orpington and this caused 1757 to show 'the white feather' at her safety valves. I soon realised why, since standing at the London end of Orpington station was Inspector Mockeridge. He raised his hand, with one finger raised upwards, showing his approval of our engine. Once under 'the bridge of sighs' we picked up speed rapidly and Jack put his injector on to bring up the level of water in the boiler. I raked coal forward on the tender, gave it a good dousing with water and continued to build up the fire for the sprint from Tonbridge to Ashford. Jack came over my side and said, 'When we pass Tonbridge starter note the time, then again passing Ashford starter', and went back to his side. I had the feeling he was going to see how fast 1757 would go, and this depended on how well I did with the shovel. Boiler full up, 180 on the clock with 1757 blowing off vigorously, we rounded the Tonbridge curve and Jack opened her out. The cut-off on 40 per cent, she roared through the station and I noted the time on my watch; then it was into her, seven shovelfuls at a time. Keep the fire bright. Watch the chimney, keep an eye on the road ahead. Check the level of water in the gauge glasses. Rake more coal forward. Spray the tender. Jack pulled the lever up to a shade over 30 per cent and that's where it stayed. Mile after mile 1757 stormed along, her exhaust shooting skyward, every now and then black smoke as I fired again and again. She seemed to like the cut-off and the firing, for the clock stayed on 180, the injector on all the way.

Pluckey distant was on. Jack hung on the whistle, regulator still open. The distant came off in time and he whistled acknowledgement. Ashford outer distant was off – we both grinned. 1757 hurried on and as we passed Ashford starter I looked at my watch – 22½ minutes point to point; we had averaged just over 70 m.p.h. 'Should have averaged 80! That's what we had to do to keep time on the 80-minute 'Folkestone Flyers' with these engines', said Jack but I think he was pleased.

We were in Westenhanger three minutes early. It was a warm morning and the tea-can had long since been emptied. We took the train onto Folkestone, then ran light to Dover loco where we put out 'L1' away. Jack took me into the local pub and I downed three pints of Kentish Ale – which was 2½ pints more than I had drunk before. I suffered no ill effects and Driver Glew commented, 'I bet it never touched the sides of your throat!'

The beginning of the summer season brought a lot more work. Preparation and disposal was a dirty job, especially for the driver, who very often had to climb into the middle of the motions to oil up, particularly on the 'Schools' with their 'middle engine' – curse of all three-cylinder classes. For the fireman's part, getting large knobs of coal from the tender and into the firebox, then shovelling a couple of tons of coal forward, was no joke on a hot summer's day. The daily scene in Bricklayers Arms loco was typical of any depot – engines all over the place, queuing for coal, fires being cleaned anywhere there was room to throw out the clinker, engines being given a 'quick clean' by the few cleaners left in the yard. And the running foremen – what a time they had. Fred Pankhurst, stub of an evil-smelling cigarette in the corner of his mouth, his battered trilby jammed on his head, would be pleading for enginemen arriving in the depot, already on overtime, to spend another two hours putting their engine away and getting it ready – and generally succeeding! Quiet-spoken Fred Gregson, 'SOS' to all and sundry, would put his arm on a fireman's shoulder and say, 'I know you have had a long day and I wouldn't blame you if you wanted to go home and leave me without your valued help in putting that little King Arthur (or Schools or whatever engine it happened to be) away for me but if you would help me I'll see to it you get paid the full overtime rate!' He, too, generally got his way. Foreman Jim Foote's approach was different again. 'One of your drivers told me he had never seen a stoker do such a good job of putting and prepping as you, my old mate! Going to show me, are you?'

The list clerk would be writing out the daily Alteration Sheet, which, with bits stuck on, would end up a yard long. Just about everybody was taken off their rostered turns so that jobs were given in strict order of seniority – a No. 4 link crew might have a Boat Train, their turn was covered by No. 6 men, whose turn would be taken by No. 8 men, and so on. One could be moved two hours either side of one's rostered time – each day if necessary, which used to make it more important than ever that, when being relieved in London, the crew looked up your next duty on the Alteration Sheet. Men living within five miles of the depot could be 'called' if a duty arose after the list clerk had gone home, or if someone was off sick. Newly-passed firemen were given a chance to show their driving skills on some of those Summer Specials but were usually hampered by having a fireman of perhaps two weeks' experience if no-one else could be found. If one of the three Running Foremen went on holiday then it was twelve-hour shifts for the two of them!

The Summer of 1948 was a good one for newly formed British Railways. The queues of people eager to sun themselves on the beaches stretched out onto the station forecourts at Victoria and Charing Cross. Travel to the Continent was booming and boat trains and relief boat trains were conjured up at very short notice. There were plenty of engines and plenty of coaching stock, but a shortage of passenger guards (cured by quick up-grading and a lot of overtime) and engine crews. Twelve hours became the normal working day, but I don't think that there were many men that would have missed it for the world.

I was talking to George Hart, our list clerk, one morning after putting away two Schools, getting them ready, then a Spam and an Arthur. 'It's about time Jack and I had a day out to the seaside!' I said, with some dignity. George screwed up his face and suggested I wait a few minutes and look at the sheet when he pinned it up. Alongside the Roster was the list of duties, so that one looked at the signing-on time and then in the Remarks column, which as we have already seen had comments like 'Pass to New Cross Gate', after which came the duty numbers. When the sheet went up I saw that I had been moved from 4 a.m. 'As Required' to 2.15 a.m., not with my own driver, but with Driver W. Thompson, an ex-New Cross man. Upon reading the duty numbers I was not pleased to see that I had the 3.23 London Bridge to Brighton newspaper train, which was booked to have an H2 Atlantic. I asked Jack Glew (who was booked to be conductor over the Old Road on the 4.50 a.m. London Bridge – Margate paper train to a New Cross man who did not know the road) how I should fire to an Atlantic. 'Like a West Country – same shape of firebox' he replied. I knew how to make up the fire for a West Country, so I determined to get in a bit early next morning and make the fire up myself. Next morning I caught the 1.15 a.m. all-night tram from Catford and arrived at the shed around 1.45 – half-hour early. The Brighton paper train engine was 'seen away' i.e. a driver and fireman did all the preparation on her, so that she was ready to step on, after reading the notices. When I got there, the two men were hard at it and welcomed my offer to make up the fire. The other fireman and myself filled the Atlantic's firebox with large knobs, right up in the back corners and under the door, letting the fire slope towards the front. The driver looked at the fire and grinned. 'Brighton this one, mate – not Birkenhead!' When Bill Thompson arrived, his first question was whether I had ever fired one of these. Upon receiving no for an answer, he looked into the box. 'Just keep her like that!' he said. No. 2424 *Beachy Head* moved quietly away at 2.30 to run light to London Bridge. We coupled on to a long line of parcel vans, four coaches, and various other vehicles which filled No. 12 Platform at London Bridge. The 3.23 did the 50½ mile sprint to Brighton in three stages – Redhill, Haywards Heath and Brighton, where she was due in at 4.47. With a fresh engine on the other end, she left at 5.00 a.m., calling at Lewes, Berwick, Polegate, Hampden Park and Eastbourne, arriving at 5.40.

Promptly at 3.23, Bill Thompson opened the regulator and sounded the thin, effeminate whistle of 2424 and we were away. He did not pull the lever up much, but this helped the fire to burn brightly and by Corbetts Lane, I started to fire. On with the injector. I sounded the whistle as we dashed through New Cross Gate and wondered whose sleep we were disturbing in the lobby of the shed engineman! 2424 was throwing a bit of fire and I got the impression that 'Bill the Basher' was not going to pull her up on the lever. Climbing the ½ mile Brockley or Forest Hill bank at 1 in 100, Bill increased the cut-off and I was shovelling for all I was worth, very glad that I had filled the box up before we left the shed. 2424 did not seem to mind and pressure remained near the 160/170 mark right up to the summit at Forest Hill. She rolled a bit, but thanks to Percy Garrish's tuition on the Mogul, I was able to get into the back corners of the firebox by twisting the shovel, thereby keeping the engine happy.

We flew down through Penge and whistled going through Norwood Junction and again at East Croydon. Bill had now notched her up and I slowed down my rate of firing. We stopped at Redhill about 3.55. Papers and mail were grabbed from the train by a little army of Post Office men and porters and prompt at 3.58, off we went. I remembered it was downhill to Horley then up to Balcombe Tunnel at 1 in 264 in each direction. I decided to stop firing at Three Bridges, which turned out to be a little premature as Bill was a bit heavy with her leaving Haywards Heath, necessitating another sharp session of firing at Wivelsfield in order to reach the final summit at the exit of Clayton Tunnel. Arriving at Brighton 'right time', it was over to Brighton loco to clean the fire and turn her. I had enjoyed my first trip on 2424 (and what proved to be my only one on an Atlantic) and Bill was mildly pleased. 'I bet it was a Brighton man who taught you how to fire to her,' was his comment. I shook my head. 'No, it was my mate, Jack Glew – a South Eastern bloke!' This remark was met with silence, then I had the sense to add, 'But Percy Garrish showed me the knack of twisting the shovel!' 'Ah, well you see now, young 'un – that is the art, getting into the back corners!' Honour satisfied, we finished our sandwiches.

We came back on the 6.24 from Brighton to London Bridge, which called at no less than 22 stations, arriving in London Bridge at 8.46, running via Lewes, Sheffield Park and Oxted. The engine was an I3, No. 2075, and made hard work of the job, especially up Freshfield bank between Sheffield Park and Horsted Keynes. We ran light to Bricklayers Arms and had time to put her away. What a morning's work!

Bill Thompson, in company with Bill Day and Bill Halliday, still proudly wore their L.B.S.C.R. cap badges and were known by us South Eastern men as the 'Brighton Bills'. Every depot had its characters and Bricklayers Arms had more than its fair share. There was driver Freddie Payne, who spoke with what was described as a toff's accent. He carried his books (rule and timetable) together with his sandwiches, in a doctor's Gladstone bag. He was nicknamed 'Doctor' Payne and rumour had it that his father was a doctor. His usual greeting when he entered the lobby was, 'Hello, chaps' and he always smiled back at some of the less gentlemanly greetings he received in exchange. Another driver used to breed pigs in his spare time and had a piggery in the space in between the Crayford Spur. He had the uncanny ability to go to sleep standing up, for example while waiting for a signal to come off. As soon as the signal was pulled, he came wide awake again. . . . Another driver used to discuss the impossibility of there being a God. He would argue vehemently with members of the Salvation Army who regularly entered 'The Swan' public house, opposite the Pages Walk entrance to the shed where Army members, both male and female, would sell copies of 'The War Cry' to us enginemen. We younger lads used to say to the Salvation Army lasses, 'It must be thirsty work trying to talk to us lot in this smoky old pub'. They would smile sweetly and answer, 'It is our duty, even if the atmosphere is a little dusty'. To this reply our answer was, 'Right then, gal, what you going to have?' The reply was always, 'A glass of water', which the publican grudgingly supplied.

To return to the atheist driver. His mate for some time was Jack Davis, at present a driver at Grove Park in South-East London, who told me this amusing anecdote. One morning, with an unfitted goods train, Davis and this driver were approaching a busy junction in the early hours, and a rare thing occurred – the vacuum brake on their C class 0–6–0 failed to hold them on the downward gradient. Worse was to come; the signals for the junction were on and even worse, another goods train was pulling out of a siding, right across their path. The disbeliever, putting his engine into reverse, looked skyward and called out, 'If there is a God watching us, please let us stop in time and I will believe!' Jack related how they went straight into the other train, scattering smashed wagons in all directions. When the dust died down, his driver turned to Jack and said, 'You see – there is no God!' To this, Jack replied, 'Who stopped us from even having a scratch?' The driver died, some years later, still an atheist – but was often referred to as 'Old Gawd Help Us'.

Boat trains were normally the jealously guarded top link duties at Stewarts Lane and Dover sheds. In the summer, however, try as they may, neither of these two depots could produce enough crews to meet the extra heavy demands of traffic. Flying to the Continent was still in its infancy and the way to go to France was by train. Contrary to popular belief, there was only one train which actually crossed the English Channel – this was the 'Night Ferry'. Many a passenger who boarded

'The Golden Arrow' was somewhat disappointed when they had to detrain at Dover and board a boat when they expected to do the whole journey in the train!

The arrivals and departures of the boats to and from France tended to 'swamp' Dover Marine and if the weather was rough, as the English Channel can be, boats tended to arrive almost together, causing more congestion. Each boat train had two paths booked – one via Tonbridge and Ashford, the other via Maidstone East, known to us by reason of its tougher gradients as 'over the mountains' – so that if a train missed its booked path due to delays at one end, an alternative path was available so as not to disrupt other services. Boat workings tended to be 'unbalanced', that is there was not a return working, and thus the trip was a one-way duty, the crew generally going down as passenger and working the train, then bringing the engine back to their home depot. On odd occasions, the duty involved working back (or down); a fireman who did well on the one trip and poorly on the return was known as a 'one-way fireman!'

One afternoon Jack Glew and I were booked 'Pass to Dover on the 3.15 from Charing Cross' and arrived in Dover loco about a quarter to six. Our engine was to be 21C170 – a Battle of Britain class named *Manston*, which we were to work up to Victoria and be relieved by Stewarts Lane men who would take her home. We made up the fire, with some lovely Kentish Betteshanger coal, and I shovelled enough forward to make sure I did not have to open the tender doors and pull some down en route. This was a filthy job and tended to happen when the fire needed all a fireman's attention. We backed onto a twelve coach train, packed with returning holiday makers. My one hope was that we would be routed via the main line and not over 'The Mountains'. Luck was with me and via the main line it was to be. Headcode boards in position, one over each buffer, the corresponding electric lamps switched on ready for when dusk fell. A large timekeeping board was then tied near the top of the smokebox, the purpose of which was to aid signalmen in giving priorities.

We had 100 minutes to do the 78 miles. It is downhill from Dover to Westenhanger at an average of 1 in 250, a slight rise of 1 in 850 into Ashford then a gentle descent at 1 in 250 to 1 in 220 to Tonbridge. 21C170 was a fine engine and with the aid of the soft Kent coal (which did not burn through too quickly but gave out a terrific heat), I managed to keep the pressure between 265–275. Jack pulled her up, though with that Bulleid reverser it was impossible to assess the correct cut-off in use. Whatever it was – probably around 20 per cent – she liked it and I noted the time passing Ashford starter. Pressure in the steam chest was reduced from 195 at Ashford to about 140 and I even had time to acknowledge the waves of trainspotters along the line, then back on the shovel. We had clear signals as far as the eye could see and there was no mistaking that Jack's intention was to beat our previous 22½ minute 'best' over this stretch. And beat it we did, passing Tonbridge (where speed had to be reduced to take the 40 m.p.h. limit round the right-hand curve, at the foot of the 1 in 120 climb up to Sevenoaks) in 19¾ minutes! Jack was pleased, adding that with an 'L1' the drivers used to take the curve nearer 50 than 40, but then an 'L1' was a 4–4–0. With a 4–6–2 Pacific, that longer wheelbase demanded better respect for the speed limit (the limit is now 50 m.p.h. officially).

Up the bank to Hildenborough, we were increasing speed steadily and 21C170 seemed hardly to notice the long climb. Through Sevenoaks and up into Polhill Tunnel we went, with Jack listening to hear if she lost her feet on the slippery rail surface in the wet tunnel; but no, she kept her feet and we burst out into the evening sunlight. Time for a wave to some nurses down in Orpington Hospital and then look ahead as Orpington station flashed by, with the inevitable inspector standing on the platform end to watch our progress, making sure to sound the hooter as we passed by him. Petts Wood distant was on, no doubt the signalman there making sure we checked down our speed for the left-hand junction we were to take into Bickley. Jack brought her down to 40 and the left-hand distant came off. Down the 1 in 96 through Bromley South – what a nasty pull away that was for down trains stopping there. I had finished firing at Knockholt, our usual place, and our speed now remained in the low forties; Kent House, nearly there now, down through the 1 in 101 Sydenham Hill Tunnel. *Manston* was blowing off steam, in spite of the low fire we now carried, whilst the water level was down to a third of a glass – plenty of room to fill her up and keep things quiet in Victoria. Jack opened the regulator and pointed to the injectors. I turned one on and the blowng-off ceased.

We ran carefully into Victoria, some two minutes early, and stopped. The passengers de-trained. Several came up to the engine and thanked Jack for a good run. Two Frenchmen came up to the cab and thanked us. I answered them in my school boy French. Their eyes lit and I realised I had made a mistake by leading them to believe I could converse with them in their own language – luckily they broke into English and explained that they were Mechaniciens off the PLM. Jack had them up into the cab and we had a long chat, without realising that no relief crew were there to relieve us. Jack, who as I stated earlier was an Improvement Class Instructor, was able to answer their technical enquiries about our engine, except one, which was, 'What was the temperature of the fire when working over the fast section?' Bullleid had not thought it necessary to have firebox pyrometers, which our French friends could not understand! Jack satisfied them by commenting, 'Well, it was bloody hot!'

Our French guests reluctantly left the footplate and we looked in vain for relief. Our empties had gone to Stewarts Lane sidings. The signal came off – we were light to Stewarts Lane loco which we reached eventually, after taking our place in a long line of incoming engines, around ten o'clock. We were due to book off at 10.30 and one was allowed an hour to get back to Bricklayers Arms from Stewarts Lane. They had not got a single set of spare men and we reluctantly had to put *Manston* away, leaving Stewarts Lane about eleven. Then, since we did not know our next turn of duty, we had to go back to 'the Brick' to look at the Alteration Sheet, since this was not up when we had booked on at 2.30. We were surprised to see we were booked to run the 3.15 Goods to Hither Green – what a comedown!

We booked on at 1.30 the next day and had hardly time to sign in the book when George Dunnett, the foreman, flew out of his office. 'Right, you two! Get up to Victoria; catch the 2.40 to Ramsgate – there is no-one booked to bring back the Guiness Brewery special from Margate this evening. And Ramsgate got one of our bloody Schools that we badly needed here!'

Jack and I agreed that this could be a far more interesting run than the 3.15 down to Hither Green, so off we went to 'the Vic' and travelled down as passenger to Ramsgate. In the loco there the Running Foreman told us that our engine was to be No. 771, a King Arthur. Jack looked at him a moment, shook his head and started to search his pockets. 'Our Running Foreman told us to bring back one of our Schools you've been hanging on to. I got her number here, somewhere.' He continued to search his pockets. This bluff worked, for the Ramsgate foreman grinned. 'Ah, yes you are the Bricklayers Arms men. I thought you were from The Lane! (Stewarts Lane) Yes, you've got to take home 934 *St. Lawrence*. She's on Two Road, all ready for you.' Jack smiled and turned to leave the foreman's office, stopping long enough to say, 'And 771 doesn't belong to Stewarts Lane, either, chum!'

Ever since 934 was built, she had been allocated to Bricklayers Arms, though Ramsgate should have been her home since the school she was named after was there. During the London Blitz, she was taken out of the blazing Cannon Street station, with a train, to save it being destroyed by fire. Driver James Foote, later to become one of the Running Foremen at Bricklayers Arms, was in charge. The engine was almost immediately struck by a bomb which severely damaged her, Foote and his fireman being lucky to escape with a scalding. The 4–4–0 being in the way of the bomb actually saved Cannon Street Bridge from destruction. For years afterwards, 934 was occasionally referred to as 'Footie's engine'. After the war, when St. Lawrence College returned home to Ramsgate from wartime evacuation, 934 was at the head of the school train. This was some of her varied history.

However, back to that summer evening in 1948. . . . After careful last-minute checks, we picked up our train of ten Maunsell coaches and ran the train 'empties to Margate'. There we stopped, topped up the tender water supply so as to have a full 4 000 gallons for the non-stop run to Victoria as well as plenty to take the engine back to the Brick. The employees of Guinness' famous brewery had had a good day at Margate – a beautiful sunny one and needless to say, plenty of their own refreshment. The loading of the crates of empty beer bottles prompted Jack to say to me, as he watched them one after another being loaded into the train, 'I could retire if I took all those empty bottles back to my local off-licence!'

The man in charge of the outing came up to us and said he would see us all right at the other end. Could he ride on the footplate, he asked, but Jack told him, only if he had a footplate pass. 'I bet you couldn't allow unauthorised persons into your brewery could you?' to which the chap agreed and made a rather unsteady return to the train. Jack grinned and commented to me, 'He's had a few.'

Non-stop runs between Margate and London were rare – *'The Thanet Belle'* Pullman stopped at Whitstable, whilst even today's electric service to the Kent Coast has no non-stop runs to Margate. We got a clear road and with our featherweight load, 934 steadily gained time. It was a glorious summer evening and we had a clear road right through and 934 (a big-chimney School) chattered along, with that lovely six beats-to-the-bar rhythm that marks a three-cylinder locomotive. Jack took out his watch – a rare event – as we passed Rochester; 'four minutes ahead of time – she obviously wants to get back home.' Some modern writers refute the idea that locomotives are all 'shes' and try to insist they should be 'its'. They might just as well try to tell the crew of

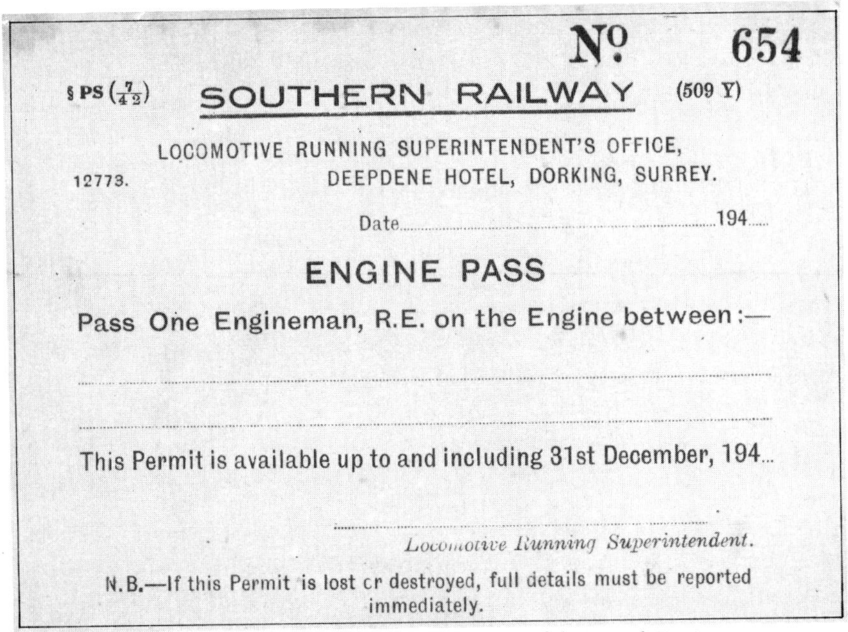

Nº 654

§ PS (7/42) **SOUTHERN RAILWAY** (509 Y)

LOCOMOTIVE RUNNING SUPERINTENDENT'S OFFICE,

12773. DEEPDENE HOTEL, DORKING, SURREY.

Date..194.....

ENGINE PASS

Pass One Engineman, R.E. on the Engine between :—

....

....

This Permit is available up to and including 31st December, 194...

....

Locomotive Running Superintendent.

N.B.—If this Permit is lost cr destroyed, full details must be reported immediately.

Footplate permit issued during the War to enginemen of the Royal Engineers.

Schools No. 30915 given the full Stewarts Lane treatment for a Royal Derby Day working. [R.H.N. Hardy]

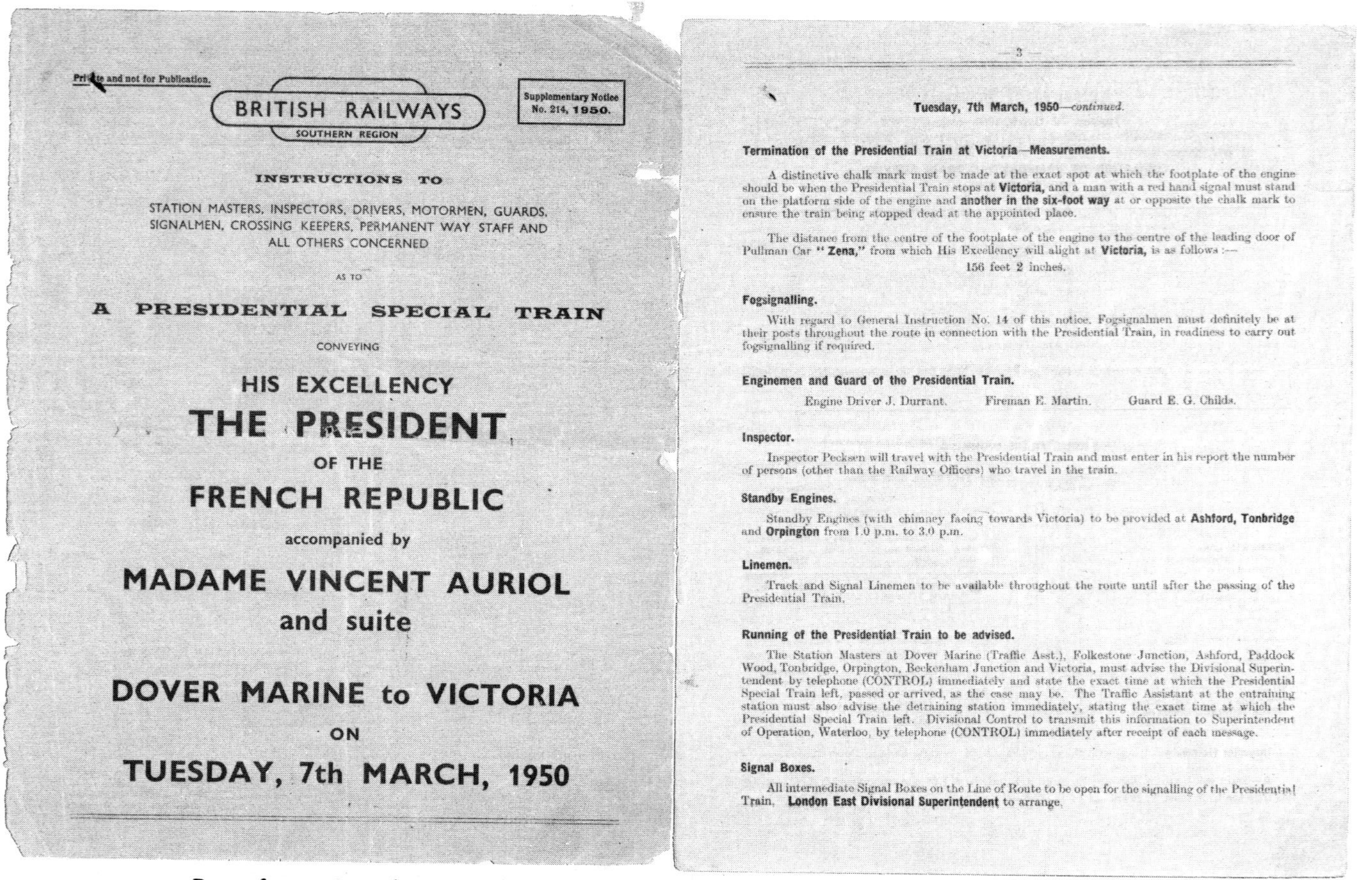

Private and not for Publication.

BRITISH RAILWAYS
SOUTHERN REGION

Supplementary Notice No. 214, 1950.

INSTRUCTIONS TO

STATION MASTERS, INSPECTORS, DRIVERS, MOTORMEN, GUARDS, SIGNALMEN, CROSSING KEEPERS, PERMANENT WAY STAFF AND ALL OTHERS CONCERNED

AS TO

A PRESIDENTIAL SPECIAL TRAIN

CONVEYING

HIS EXCELLENCY
THE PRESIDENT
OF THE
FRENCH REPUBLIC
accompanied by
MADAME VINCENT AURIOL
and suite

DOVER MARINE to VICTORIA
ON
TUESDAY, 7th MARCH, 1950

— 3 —

Tuesday, 7th March, 1950—*continued.*

Termination of the Presidential Train at Victoria—Measurements.

A distinctive chalk mark must be made at the exact spot at which the footplate of the engine should be when the Presidential Train stops at **Victoria,** and a man with a red hand signal must stand on the platform side of the engine and **another in the six-foot way** at or opposite the chalk mark to ensure the train being stopped dead at the appointed place.

The distance from the centre of the footplate of the engine to the centre of the leading door of Pullman Car "**Zena,**" from which His Excellency will alight at **Victoria,** is as follows:—

156 feet 2 inches.

Fogsignalling.

With regard to General Instruction No. 14 of this notice, Fogsignalmen must definitely be at their posts throughout the route in connection with the Presidential Train, in readiness to carry out fogsignalling if required.

Enginemen and Guard of the Presidential Train.

Engine Driver J. Durrant. Fireman E. Martin. Guard E. G. Childs.

Inspector.

Inspector Pecksen will travel with the Presidential Train and must enter in his report the number of persons (other than the Railway Officers) who travel in the train.

Standby Engines.

Standby Engines (with chimney facing towards Victoria) to be provided at **Ashford, Tonbridge** and **Orpington** from 1.0 p.m. to 3.0 p.m.

Linemen.

Track and Signal Linemen to be available throughout the route until after the passing of the Presidential Train.

Running of the Presidential Train to be advised.

The Station Masters at Dover Marine (Traffic Asst.), Folkestone Junction, Ashford, Paddock Wood, Tonbridge, Orpington, Beckenham Junction and Victoria, must advise the Divisional Superintendent by telephone (CONTROL) immediately and state the exact time at which the Presidential Special Train left, passed or arrived, as the case may be. The Traffic Assistant at the entraining station must also advise the detraining station immediately, stating the exact time at which the Presidential Special Train left. Divisional Control to transmit this information to Superintendent of Operation, Waterloo, by telephone (CONTROL) immediately after receipt of each message.

Signal Boxes.

All intermediate Signal Boxes on the Line of Route to be open for the signalling of the Presidential Train. **London East Divisional Superintendent** to arrange.

Pages from a Special Notice relating to the working of a Presidential Special Train from Dover Marine to Victoria. *[Author's Collection]*

a ship that they serve in an 'it' and not a 'she' as convince a locomotive man that an engine has always been referred to as she – even though her name be *Lord Nelson, King Arthur* or *Sir Nigel Gresley*.

Rochester station, then as now, is situated on a sharp curve after which comes the Sole Street bank, five miles of climbing at 1 in 100, after which the road undulates to within two miles of Bromley South; there the road drops down at 1 in 95 to the station, then up and down to Shortlands, then up at 1 in 101 to Kent House, down at 1 in 330 through Penge Tunnel, followed by two miles down the 1 in 101 to Brixton, finishing with the 1 in 64 descent of Grosvenor Bridge into Victoria. Stopping there, just five minutes ahead of time, 934 had 'eaten the timetable'.

The gentleman who had come up to us at Margate again made an unsteady approach and succeeded in climbing up onto the footplate to shake our hands. Then two of his colleagues deposited a number of full bottles onto the footplate. The tool-bucket was filled up with cold water and several wipers were wrapped around the bottles, to stop them knocking against each other on our journey back to the shed. Jack and I agreed that it had been a good day and we drank to the health of the brewery and to 934!

Jack and I had several 'Ferry Vans' to Dover with a King Arthur which 'ate the job', as it demanded a mere 40 m.p.h. to keep time. The summer was soon over and it was time for me to move up the links and leave Jack Glew who, in the relatively short time I had been his fireman, had taught me so much. I moved into No. 5 link, and for a short while I had a driver whom I will refer to as 'Old Jawhard'. He was an ex-South Eastern man who, like my grandfather, considered that firemen no longer existed – 'They all died years ago.'

My first day with him was unforgettable. He drew a line with his boot from the centre of the firehole door to the centre of the shovelplate, saying to me 'That's your half – keep to it!' I took this at first as a joke, since some of the firemen were unable to fire with either hand and had to stand on the driver's side of the footplate in order to fire. A Schools, for example, needed a fireman who could fire with the shovel in his left hand (since the driver stood on the left side. A fireman who was not ambidextrous was called 'a left-handed fireman' or a 'right-handed fireman' and on small engines frequently got in the driver's way when standing on his side of the footplate to fire). I answered pleasantly enough, 'That won't be necessary. I can fire with either hand, driver!' He looked at me coldly and said witheringly, 'I expect you to be able to fire properly but the only time you come over my side is to sweep the footplate or clean my cab-lights.' After this, he did not speak to me for the rest of the duty, other than a grunt which I took for 'Good Night' when we left the depot. . . .

The second week with my talkative mate was the 10.15 from Bricklayers Arms to Tonbridge, via Maidstone. As mentioned earlier, Old Jawhard's side of the footplate was his alone, but on the first trip out that week, we had a cleaner aboard as third man for this 'running trip' prior to taking up firing duties. This youngster made the mistake of climbing onto the engine from the driver's side! He was icily told to get down, walk round the engine and get up on the stoker's side – and to keep there!

I made up a big fire on the 'C' class 0–6–0 we were on and got the cleaner to help me throw coal forward on the tender. The driver walked away from the engine to get a clean wiper. The cleaner looked apprehensive – as well he might. 'Are all the drivers like 'im?' he enquired of me. I had to laugh. 'No chum! He's a one-off, in a class of his own!' 'Thank Gawd for that!' came the reply.

We had a medium load of 45 plus a brake and I let the cleaner have the shovel when we left Blackheath.

One or two small pieces of coal fell onto the driver's foot. He looked at the young cleaner, then down at the coal, then resumed his driving stance without a word. I handed the cleaner the brush; he swept up the spilt coal and, as an afterthought, lightly brushed the toe of the driver's boot, to remove the coal dust. Even now, I still cannot make up my mind if this was done to placate or irritate Old Jawhard!

The third week was an 'H' Class tank duty. Taking empty coaches from Cannon Street, via Metropolitan Junction up the sharp climb to Ludgate Hill Station, run round, then down to Blackheath Carriage Sidings via Nunhead and Lewisham. We stood at Blackheath for about two hours, then took the same route back to Cannon Street, after which we went back to the Brick and put her away. This time-wasting routine was typical due to the lack of suitable stabling points for coaching stock, which had to be moved out of the inner London Area as quickly as possible, but in order not to interfere with the heavy electric train services, the 'roundabout' route was necessary. My driver really pasted our 'H' up the bank from Met. Junction and she dropped back from 160 to 140. I got a stony stare and the lever dropped further over for my pains.

As this was a front shift duty, I wondered what the next week would bring and on the Saturday afternoon, when we had finished putting the engine away, I looked at the Roster Sheet and found that my driver's name had been rubbed out and that of 'C. Dickinson' put in its place. Old Jawhard had been put into the 'Tankie' Gang, since he had just reached retiring age and, as it turned out, had requested to be transferred to what was irreverently termed 'The Old Men's Gang'.

CHAPTER FOUR

Banking, Shunting and Specials

Charlie Dickinson was the reverse of my previous driver. A short jovial man, with a reddish face, generally smiling. Our first job together was Angerstein Wharf pilot, for which a Brighton 'E1' tank was provided. To a New Cross man, these engines were known as 'Black Tanks', but due to their ability to dash about, the South Eastern fraternity dubbed them 'Rooters'. To a New Cross man a 'Rooter' was an AIX, more commonly known as 'Terriers'.

Our Rooter was No. 2151, standing in the bombed-out open space known as the New Shed. I started to move the turntable into position, while Charlie boarded 2151, turned on the 'Donkey' pump, opened the cylinder cocks and put her into forward gear. He touched the whistle, from which a spray of water was ejected. A mere touch on the regulator and 2151, spraying steam and water in all directions, made a startlingly brisk approach to the turntable, which I had only just about got into position. A loud yell came from Charlie on the footplate. 'The little sod is running away with me, Mick! Do something!' 2151 bounced onto the turntable, and I had visions of her running obliquely across the Hay Road and into the breakdown crane. I managed to scramble onto the footplate and help Charlie throw the lever into reverse. 2151 then shot backwards from the turntable and down into the New Shed. Repeated applications of the Westinghouse brake did little to slow her down, so into forward gear we went and headed again for the turntable. Charlie put her into mid-gear, opened the regulator wide and slammed it shut. Brakes on once again and finally 2151 stood, docile as a lamb, in the centre of the turn-table, steam pouring from her cylinder cocks. Sweat was running down our faces, for a runaway engine is no joke. The firelighters had lit her up with a full boiler of water, which we reckoned had caused the regulator to be choked and unable to be shut. How wrong we were! Once into the Old Shed, we had six attempts to stop her right for water. No. 2151 wanted to be on the move alright, all the time. Charlie Dickinson told me to go and see the foreman who, at that moment, appeared by the side of the engine to see what was going on. It was Jim Foote, and he looked up at the pair of us as we screwed the handbrake on as hard as it would go. 'Staying for dinner, Charlie?' he enquired. Dinner was served in the canteen at noon – it was now 7.30 – we were due away and would lose our path in the timetable if we remained much longer.

'This one's a bloody menace, Jim – she won't stand still', rejoined my mate. Jim climbed onto the footplate and said 'Take her down through the shed, Charlie'. We released the handbrake and once into forward gear, without even touching the regulator, 2151 made a fair impression of a horse leaving the starting gates at Epsom. Jim helped my driver to put her in reverse and after another move in the forward direction, the 'H' was again brought to a stand, cylinder cocks open, lever in mid-gear. Jim Foote climbed down. 'Regulator gland blowing through! I'll get a couple of "As Required" men to relieve you and we'll shed this blighter. Take 2128 on Six Road and get down to Angersteins as soon as you can. I shall be having a few words with the men who put her away'. Charlie thanked him, adding, 'If I'd taken her to Angersteins, me and my mate would have finished up shunting at Silvertown for the L.N.E.R.!' – Silvertown being on the opposite side of the River Thames to Angerstein Wharf.

Such was our first day together. Angersteins received material for use in the London Transport tram and trolleybus Central Repair Depot at Charlton Works, situated adjacent to Angersteins, and one of the pilot's duties was to shunt wagons for the C.R.D. into their sidings. There were bits and pieces of old trams lying in the yard which today would be prized possessions in a museum and, to add spice to the proceedings, many of the sidings had no buffer stops, so that shunting was carried out at a much slower speed than was customary at other locations.

A week or so later, we were shunting at New Cross Gate and had two trips up Forest Hill bank, as banking engine. We had an E5, No.

2590, a type which our ex-New Cross colleagues referred to as 'Large Radials'. Our first trip up the bank was uneventful – if one could call normal 2½ miles at full regulator, with a 40 per cent cut-off, sparks coming down 'with ice on them' and the shovel rattling furiously in and out of those awkward tip-flap doors! Our second trip was a little more inspiring. This duty was to provide banking assistance for the train known as 'The Hornby' – hauled by one of the three very powerful electric locomotives nicknamed 'Hornbys' by all and sundry. I made the fire right up, putting every large knob of coal I could find into the back corners and under the door. We filled the side tanks with water and waited in the adjacent road until the train was marshalled. The Hornby backed on, the load being 65 and a brake. Steam roared from the E5's safety valves, ready for that long climb up Forest Hill bank. Sounding her electric train chime-whistle, the Hornby pulled out of the sidings at a steadily increasing speed. 'He can't have them all hooked on, Mick', said Charlie as the train accelerated by on the next road to us; but we saw the guard exchange handsignals with the 'fireman' (these electrics carried a fireman to hook up and un-couple and when running passenger trains, (usually the Newhaven boat trains) the fireman looked after the electrically heated boiler, which provided steam heating for the train. From these easy duties stemmed another quip aimed at a fireman who could not keep up a good head of steam, viz. 'My mate is a good fireman – on the bloody Hornby!' – though being a fireman on the Hornby was only one turn in their steam roster of normal firing duties, at Newhaven Shed. Well, the guard's brake van finally went by and Charlie waited for the shunter to give us the correct green light to follow the train. The shunter must have thought he had done so, but we saw nothing; after a few moments Charlie sounded the whistle. The shunter gave the green light plus some other urgent oral and visual signals to Charlie, and we were off. The lights of the brake van were, by now, some way away, with the driver of the electric notching up and picking up speed as if he were running light-engine and not with 65 wagons behind him! Charlie opened up poor old 2590 and we raced after the disappearing train we were supposed to be banking. We caught up with it at Brockley and just managed to touch the buffers of the brake van, the guard hanging out on the back verandah laughing and holding out his hand in encouragement for us to keep up with him! Sparks from our chimney rained down on him as he was having a good smile at our efforts to keep up with, let alone bank, the Hornby. We did manage to give him a bit of a push going through Honor Oak Park but that was about all. . . .

We stopped in Forest Hill station and I changed the two red banking tail lights for one white light in the middle of the buffers to signify 'light to New Cross Gate'. Then we went over the crossover near to the old coal yard and opposite to where the old Croydon Railway atmospheric pumping house had once stood. Here the Croydon Railway banking engines also used to cross over, with their two red tail lights, before they too returned light to New Cross many years before.

'Well!' laughed Charlie, 'that was exciting! What shall we do for an encore?' I grinned and said, 'Well, we could double-head the Brighton Mail!'

Summer over, the hop picking season was under way and Bricklayers Arms provided the motive power for the hop pickers' trains – usually referred to as 'oppers specials. Old South Eastern and Chatham stock which for most of the years stood in the rusty Sidings at Maze Hill, Blackheath and other locations, was taken out to run these specials, as well as those for the 'hop pickers' friends, who used to go down to visit the families working in the Garden of England – or to be more specific, the hop gardens of Kent. Paddock Wood was the centre of the hopping industry, with such stations as Yalding, Marden, Staplehurst and Headcorn receiving very many thousands of willing hands who spent their summer fortnight picking the basis of their favourite beverage. In the 1940s, holidays with pay were the exception rather than the rule and many families worked on hop picking more for the money than the fresh air.

To avoid interfering with the regular and boat train traffic, the routes of some of the Hoppers was what could only be described as 'interesting'. As one driver put it, 'They only sent us this roundabout way to see if the points and signals still work!' If the carriages were ancient – and they were – the engines allocated were of similar vintage. The Old Croydon Shed at New Cross was emptied and unrebuilt 'D' class Coppertops were cleaned up and made ready, to spend a few more weeks on the road before being put back into store.

Our first trip was with No. 1746 and a real rusty state she was in. The cleaners had had a go but she did not look much better. Still, she had to do. Our destination was Pluckley, then take the empties to Ashford and into the loco there. Looking at the duty details, Charlie commented, 'I don't believe it!' I saw that we were routed via Forest Hill, South Croydon Junction, Oxted, round the little used Crowhurst spur through Edenbridge and join the Kent main line at Tonbridge! I made sure of plenty of coal forward for what with Forest Hill Bank to climb, then uphill at 1 in 100 all the way to Hurst Green from South Croydon Junction, it was going to be a hard run. For some reason we could never understand, the Hoppers were timed very tightly, leaving no margins for engines that had not been 'run in' after their long periods of storage.

We left London Bridge, Low Level, and Charlie opened up our steed, which he had oiled up – twice, all over. She was very stiff. I put the injector on as we passed by Shuttleworths and knew it would have to stay on, since the 19″ × 26″ cylinders used steam, and consequently water, at an alarming rate. The boiler was a good steam producer, but the injectors of the Coppertops were on the slow side and when worked really hard, both had to be used for short periods in order to maintain a decent level of water, which tended to 'knock back' the steam pressure from the prescribed 175 p.s.i.

Through New Cross Gate I had a chance to sound the lovely Wainwright whistle and Charlie had really got the poor old girl moving along. We had some decent coal, Yorkshire Hards, and we had all the steam we needed going up Forest Hill bank. Once over the top, on went that second injector on the slightly downhill run to East Croydon. With the boiler full, both injectors came off as we swung round the left-hand curve at South Croydon Junction, then regulator wide open for the long climb up through Oxted. On with the injector, seven shovelfuls every half mile, with the cut-off rasping on 40 per cent. What a firework display that ascent would have been at night! But the sun shone and we were both sweating; in fact if I remember correctly, the tea can was empty as we ran through Oxted.

By Hurst Green, the water was in the bottom nut of the gauge glass so on went that second injector and back went the pressure – 170, 165, 160, but at last Hurst Green Halt was passed and the worst was over. When we stopped at Paddock Wood, a man and his family trooped up to the engine, a bottle of brown ale in his hand; he took a swig from the bottle and grinned at us! Thanks for the ride, driver! Me and the missus picked a lovely bunch of flowers as we went through Oxted!' and off he went. 'There's gratitude, Mick, I hope the weather. . . .'. His last words were drowned as our engine blew off steam.

Our second 'hop picker' was routed via Lewisham, Catford Bridge and Selsdon, then up over the Oxted heights to Edenbridge, coming back onto the main line at Tonbridge. I commented something to the effect that they could not send us a more devious way round to Paddock Wood, but of course, I was wrong. Our very next duty was via

New Cross, Blackheath, up through Falconwood, Dartford, then over the twisty route from Strood, Maidstone West and Yalding to end up at Paddock Wood, facing the way we had come!

Our last Hopper together was a memorable one. Upon reading the duty Charlie said to me, 'Blimey! They must have made a mistake! We are booked to run to Pluckley via our own main line – Orpington and Sevenoaks!' I was pleased – get to bridge No. 179 and it was all over – a piece of cake. Fred Gregson was on duty and I enquired what locomotive he had for us. He smiled – and when Fred smiled it usually meant he found the situation amusing for all the wrong reasons. 'You have got an Ashford engine, working home – No. 1711!' I thanked Fred and walked through the Old Shed, looking for a rebuilt Coppertop. I could not see one on the road Fred had told me and I looked again. Charlie was beside me. 'There she is, Mick – 1711!' I stared. There she was alright, no rebuilt Coppertop but a 'C' class 0–6–0 – with 5 '2' driving wheels on a fast 'Hopper'. . . . I could not help repeating the phrase that Driver Garrish had used when, only a few short months ago, I had informed him that I had been firing for two weeks; I stared at the 'C' Class and murmured, 'Oh, my good Gawd!' Charlie slapped me on the back and said, 'That's all we used to get on the Ramsgate excursions when I was firing, Mick! I'll show you how we used to do it'. And he did. He got me up on the tender, to throw onto the footplate every large knob of coal I could see. He threw these into the firebox until the coal almost, but not quite, reached the brick-arch. We then went onto the coal road and had a ton or so of small coal to fill up the tender at the front end. I looked at the fire. It looked almost out. Charlie told me to tighten the smokebox door and then sit down while we ran light to London Bridge. Running up, he opened the cut-off and 'laced her' all the way. At first the steam dropped from 140 to 120 and I thought, 'That's it!' We haven't even got a train on and she's on the floor! But of course, Charlie knew exactly what he was doing. By the time we had hooked on, made a brake, chatted with the guard, 1711 was near blowing off. I filled the boiler, shut off the injector. 'Right Away' and Charlie opened her gently and off we went. He glanced at the fire. 'Give her six at a time when we get by Peak Freans, she'll be as good as gold'. Once through St. John's, the climb started, but I was pleasantly surprised at the speed Charlie had coaxed out of our 'C' 'over the arches' towards New Cross. A 30 per cent cut-off and we were already at Hither Green. Injector singing away, fire-hole doors two inches open, 160 on the clock – full working pressure. Six more into the fire, which was white hot, just a few inches below the glaring white brick-arch.

By Orpington, I had the firehole doors half-open, steam whimpering at the valves and the injector still singing away. As was to be expected, Inspector Mockeridge was waiting on the platform and Charlie eased the regulator, allowing 1711 to blow off as we tore through. 'That will show him – we Bricklayers Arms men can run any engine!' We had a marvellous trip down and when we took her into Ashford loco. and were relieved by P & D men, her brick arch was still glowing!

To digress, a short while ago, my works outing included a trip on the Bluebell Line and I was given the privilege of having the shovel on 'C' class No. 592. To my surprise, the driver said she was a bit of a shy steamer. I filled the box to within eighteen inches of the brick arch, sat on the fireman's seat and thereafter just worked the injector now and again! Charlie's method still worked!

A re-arrangement in the links, due to the last influx of New Cross men, resulted in my losing Charlie Dickinson as my driver. In the short time I had with him, I learned a lot that helped to make me a more competent fireman. My new driver was Ted Biggs, a tall neat man, whose personal tidiness was always reflected in his work. We had a couple of 'hop picker' trains, then it was late autumn and much P & D (Preparation and Disposal) work and shunting duties, mainly at New Cross Gate, came our way. Ted had a deep mistrust of Brighton relics and was not pleased when he learned that our third week together was going to be on the Tattenham Goods, with a C2X 0–6–0 'Vulcan'. He disliked the pant-pant of the Westinghouse 'Donkey' pump on Brighton engines, referring to it as 'that incessant two-note tune'. For the pleasure of running the Tattenham Goods, one signed on at 2.15 a.m., got the engine ready, then light to New Cross Gate. A banking engine was usually provided since the train was a heavy one, of a type long since gone, namely the 'pick-up' goods. We stopped at Norwood Junction, Purley, Reedham, Chipstead, Kingswood and Tattenham Corner. Climb Forest Hill Bank, then from East Croydon, after stopping at Norwood Junction, it was 1 in 264 all the way to Purley, down to Reedham, then up 1 in 100 to Kingswood, through Hoppity Tunnel and Tadworth station to Tattenham Corner. By the time we had shunted at each stop, it was 6 a.m. and time to work our way back to Reedham, where we stood and waited to be relieved by Norwood men around 9 a.m. Naturally, Ted Biggs oiled her while I cleaned the fire and threw coal forward, since the Norwood men had a lot more work to do with the Vulcan after they relieved us.

N Class No. 1823 was the first loco I cleaned. Later on, I fired her down to Three Bridges.

My first firing duty was on E4 class No. 2463 – seen here at New Cross loco.

Trains from Tattenham were still crowded with office workers, so we used to ride in the motorman's cab up to London Bridge. I watched, quite fascinated by the ease at which the motorman ran the train and the smooth operation of the Westinghouse brake.

On the Wednesday, the motorman got off his seat at Norwood Junction and said to me, 'Do you reckon you could take her to our next stop at New Cross Gate?' I hesitated. Ted said, 'He's always telling me how good the Westinghouse brake is! Go on, Mick'. So I sat down. After all, I had two experienced drivers beside me to see that I did nothing wrong. 'Right away' from the guard. Release the brakes. Put the key into 'forward', pull the 'dead man's handle' to the centre of my chest (into series) and seeing we had both home and distant in the clear, kept the handle pressed down. There were no speedometers on those old 3 SUB units, but we went through Annerley at a smart rate. 'Give her the lot now, mate,' commanded the motorman and I pushed the handle round to parallel. The rail joints thundered past beneath our feet as the power bogies accelerated up the gentle rise to Forest Hill, my home station. Now it was down 1 in 100 all the way to New Cross Gate. 'Shut off and let her run – but keep the handle down,' came the instructions. I shut off, keeping the handle down. (To release it, even in the off position, would immediately apply the brake – and re-arrange the seated and standing passengers into heaps). Now was to come the moment of truth; could I judge correctly so as to halt at the stopping mark at New Cross Gate? Brockley whizzed by. I gripped the brake handle firmly with my left hand and gave her 10 lbs of air. The train checked down immediately and I released the brakes, putting the handle back into the running position. The rail-joint beats were slower now. Passing the carriage siding on my right, the motorman advised, 'Another five, mate,' and she checked down obediently. We entered the station at a slowly decreasing rate, stopping just about right. I gave her ten and we stopped smartly. 'Key off – then you can let go the handle,' said the motorman finally. I found my hands were wet with sweat. Ted laughed. 'Poor old Mick! He was holding that handle so hard, I thought he was going to pull it off the box.'

Saturday morning, when offices still worked until mid-day, it was business as usual, but at New Cross Gate I was again told I could 'take her on up'. I made a very steady approach to London Bridge – too steady and lost half-a-minute! Such were my first experiences on the handle. . . .

We were back shift the following week, shunting at New Cross Gate.

Friday night our names were on the Alteration Sheet. Ted was booked as Pilotman to Hither Green to a New Cross driver, who did not know the road. I was booked with a driver named Taffy Hughes on the afternoon goods from Norwood Junction to Bricklayers Arms. Taffy had done the duty many times before and told me it was a 'quiet Saturday afternoon out'. We relieved Norwood men in the yard there ('the Madhouse' we used to call it, because the pilot engines there never seemed to stand still for a moment.) In fact, Norwood Yard was the first on the Southern to receive diesel-electric shunting locomotives, in 1937, which thereafter carried out most of the shunting work. I walked along the framing of the Vulcan and, after switching off the Westinghouse pump I undid the top nut to check the oil level. It appeared full to the top, so I carefully screwed back the nut and returned to the footplate. My few weeks at New Cross Gate had impressed on me the necessity to keep the pump working, so I turned it on again. We were tender first to the Brick and as was usual, when having to run tender-first, it was pouring with rain. We got the right away and set off. The Vulcans were a strong little engine, though not as strong as our 'C' class, but our load was only some 40 odd wagons, so no problem. Taffy told me he would not run too fast since on most Saturdays, 12-car electric trains crossed from the down sidings into the up for cleaning at New Cross Gate and tended to hold up the goods if it was running early. We duly reached Forest Hill and screwed on the tender handbrake as we started to descend the bank. Suddenly, Taffy remarked, 'Hey! The music has stopped!' Our Donkey Pump had stopped working. Taffy had seen me check it before starting, so suggested I took a spanner, had a short walk along the framing and give the pump a tap. This treatment usually got them going again. I suppose we were only doing 25 mph, so off I went. One light tap should do it. No. A heavier tap – nothing. Taffy leaned around the cab and yelled 'Hurry up, boyo! There must be a leak in the reservoir. We've only got 25 lbs of air left!' I hit the top of the donkey really hard, but still no movement. We were now approaching Honor Oak Park signalbox. Taffy sounded the 'cock-crow' emergency signal. The signalman waved but continued to lean on his levers, impervious to our plight. Taffy told me to tap open the pump drain-cock, expecting a flow of water, indicating the pump was empty of oil. I took the oil can and returned to the pump. 'Don't lose the top nut,' Taffy shouted after me, 'or she'll never go!' Speed had increased to near 40 m.p.h. as I opened the drain-cock. Oil ran out. The pump was full of oil – it had failed; though how, we had no time to find out. The cock-crow whistle was sounded as we passed Brockley box but I had no time to look at the signalman as I made my way alongside the boiler, the rain still pouring down, back to the footplate.

New Cross Gate distant was on. A worried but still calm Taffy scratched his chin. 'I hadn't planned on learning to play my national instrument, the harp, so soon, Mick, but if that 12-car is crossing over, we have no chance of stopping!' I had been thinking about that possibility myself. 'I'll put her in reverse and put on steam. When we enter the station, jump off! I'll be right behind you!" Watching the track whizzing by beneath the cab steps, I'm afraid the idea of jumping off did not appeal to me at all. . . .

Taffy sounded the cock-crow long and loud as we neared New Cross Gate outer. Mercifully, the 12-car had stopped halfway to the junction. New Cross Gate starter was flung into the 'clear' position and we were signalled clear onto the branch. With the lever in reverse, we had slowed but Taffy decided not to put steam on yet. We had a clear road, the signalmen had obviously realised we were a run-away and given the 4–5–5 (train running away in right direction) bell signal ahead. If Taffy put on steam in reverse, he could blow the cylinder covers and render us helpless. So, we hammered the tender hand-brake on as hard as it would go. What the guard was doing, we did not know. Down onto the branch we shot, signalled into the Sorting Siding. Taffy gave her a bit of steam and in this fashion we slowed down and finally came to a stop way up the yard. Both of us were soaked with the rain and with sweat, and I may say very glad to be in one piece. The guard walked by and called up 'Smart run down, driver! Didn't know you men could run a Vulcan like that!' At that same moment the Donkey pump came back into life and Taffy and I burst into laughter. 'You and your quiet Saturday afternoon out!' was a standing joke for years between us.

I forgot to mention that soon after Ted Biggs became my driver, I had a note from Ernie Baughen, the genial Stores chief, to go and see him. As messenger, I had fetched and carried bits and pieces for 'Ernie's stores' and had got on very well with him. Baughen had lost a leg when, as a cleaner, he was run over by an engine. I went in to see him. A large parcel was on his desk. 'That's for you,' he said, then opened his drawer and handed me my gold-coloured Engineman S.R. cap badge. In the parcel was a new serge jacket, cap and long mackintosh. I had completed 313 firing turns. I came out of the office holding my badge and passing me was Jack Glew. The metal was a fine mottled finish. 'Better get some wet sand on that and get rid of the pimples,

Mike, and you could be taken for a fireman!' Coming from an engineman like Jack, that was a compliment which I was pleased with.

Incidentally, in the wearing of grease-top caps (kept shiny by a light application of engine oil) there were 'styles'. South Eastern men favoured the top of the cap pulled back from the peak. Brighton men favoured the top pulled down over each side of the hat band. There was a strap around the top of the peak which could be fastened under the chin to avoid the cap blowing off one's head at speed. I only knew of two firemen who used it. One was always scornfully referred to by his driver as the 'bloke with the Boy Scout chin strap' – after the style of the wide-brimmed hats first introduced by Baden-Powell and secured by a similar strap. The second fireman was scathingly known by his mate as 'the stoker who wears his hat like a bloody W.R.E.N.'

A rare fashion was cap on back to front, usually adopted by drivers of some West Country class engines. This style was known as 'Paris Main Line' after French enginemen who often wore their caps back to front – a good idea really. Some firemen, myself included, copied the French idea of wearing motor cycle goggles to keep coal dust out of the eyes. One driver in the top link at the Brick wore his goggles, when not in use, up over his cap badge and earned the nickname 'Driver Rommel', after the German general. In fact Inspectors forbade the wearing of goggles since they were classed as glasses, which in those days, were not allowed to be worn by footplate staff (other than drivers who were 'Yard Duty Only', i.e. not allowed on the running lines. Today, steam enginemen are provided with safety goggles to wear by order of the Department of the Environment – how times change!

Before leaving Driver Taffy Hughes, we had another little adventure together when working our Rest Day. Again Norwood was the scene. Snowing hard, we stopped to take water with yet another Vulcan. The water pipe was a little short to go very far into the opening in the tender. Taffy turned on the water rather too hard and in no time at all I found the pipe coming out. I yelled for him to turn off – I was jumping up and down on the tender, trying to get the pipe in and getting soaked in the process. Taffy was laughing helplessly as he tried to turn off the water. I let go the pipe as the icy cold water swamped me, causing it to swing back and come to rest above Taffy. He in turn had a cold shower until he managed to turn off the water. Tender-first back to the shed our overalls froze stiff but, strange to relate, neither of us caught a cold!

With the approach of Christmas, the Southern used to run numerous 'Parcels specials' and these were usually an 'H' class 0–4–4 tank duty.

Ted Biggs told me to make up the fire, then break all the pieces of coal into sizes no bigger than a clenched fist. We then topped up the bunker with more coal and went out bunker-first. Our first Parcels was from London Bridge all stations via Greenwich to Blackheath via Slades Green – twenty stops! The reason for running bunker-first was that all these stations had their platforms on the driver's side (the right-hand side of an H, running chimney-first) necessitating the engine to run backwards. This made it easier for the driver to stop or pull up as directed by the station staff. We followed an all-stations to Dartford electric and cleared the Greenwich line when onto the Crayford Spur. At the end of this monotonous trip I asked Ted why we were not booked to run via Blackheath round to Greenwich which would have let us run chimney first, avoiding the constant coal-dust blown back into the cab by running in reverse. Ted shook his head and replied, 'Well I guess that would have made it too easy, Mick'. By the time we reached Blackheath, our coal was nearly all gone and we were pleased when we ran into Rotherhithe Road, left our empties there and ran into the loco. We filled up with coal and then up to London Bridge and did another round trip. What an evening's work!

Saturday evening we were rostered to shunt at New Cross Gate but the List Clerk thought otherwise. Ted got an evening learning the road to Brighton whilst I was given the job few No. 1 or 3 link firemen wanted – down with the 7.15 p.m. Charing Cross to Dover, arriving there at 8.58, then back up with the 9.28 ex Margate 'Mail' arriving at Dover Priory at 10.31 and departing at 10.38, calling at Folkestone Junction and the Central, fast to Ashford, then Tonbridge and via the 'Old Road' calling at Redhill and East Croydon, arriving at London Bridge at 1.19 a.m. Sunday morning. The reason it was unpopular was that on Saturday nights, the all-night trams did not run and the last train down the Lewisham and Welling route to Barnehurst left at 1.8 a.m. and the last Greenwich line train home left at 1.11 a.m.! Since quite a few enginemen lived on these routes or at Catford or Downham, many were the requests to change duties with men willing to make their own way home. Living as I did at Forest Hill, I decided that I would take my bicycle with me, on the engine tender. Going down, we had a West Country and by the time we reached Dover, the bicycle was half way down the tender, buried in coal. Coming back, it was snowing hard and bitterly cold. My cycle was placed on the roomy tender of King Arthur class No. 795 *Sir Dinadan*, and on time we left Dover for the return journey. My driver was Bert Longhurst, who lived at Mottingham but had a motor bike to get home on.

Leaving Tonbridge, we started on the 19 mile-run to Redhill. I put the injector on and since Bert was not heavy handed, knew the fire would be all right for a while, so I started to rake coal forward into the 'hole' made since leaving Dover. After a few minutes of this I remembered the injector and grabbed hold of the wheel, giving it an almighty tug to turn it off. Unbeknown to me, however, Bert had already done this and the small finger of my left hand was broken with the force I used. I was in agony and let out a yell. Bert saw what I had done in the glare of the fire and told me to put my hand onto the handbrake. I did so and he hit my small finger with the edge of his hand, so straightening it, and most of the pain went. He tied a wiper round the last two fingers of my hand as a makeshift splint and I carried on firing. This finger on my left hand is still slightly bent, a reminder of the Dover Mail and the quick thinking of Bert Longhurst – and of No. 795 *Sir Dinadan*, (of which Triang-Hornby produced a replica some 30 years later on). As a postscript, when London Bridge was reached, our relief tried to take my bicycle off the tender, but it was frozen solidly to the coal; we had to empty buckets of hot water over it before I was able to ride home . . .

Another Saturday night to Sunday morning job was what were known as Engineers' trains – track re-laying work mainly. These were booked for twelve hours and with Sunday night rate certainly made the pay packet a good one. Two weeks after my accident on the mail train, Ted and I were booked 4.15 p.m. Saturday afternoon. We prepared our engine, a 'C' class, and arrived with double measures of footplate tea. (Recipe note: two heaped teaspoonfuls of tea, four of condensed milk, stirred together to make a sticky paste, wrapped in greaseproof paper – placed, paper and all, in the tea-can, pour on boiling water, remove paper. This made one 'measure'). Sandwiches, cakes, an egg, knob of lard and rasher of bacon, plus two pieces of bread each. At 5.15 we were light to New Cross Gate Engineers' Sidings to pick up our train, a guard's brake van at each end. We provided the guard with coal and two scoopfuls of fire for each of his vans. At 6 p.m. the platelayers and foreman arrived, tea was made in the shunters' cabin, loads checked and at 7 p.m. off we went, back to North Kent West, ran round the train then right away to Knockholt. It was snowing hard and we had the cab-sheet up between the engine and the tender, which helped to keep out the biting east wind. Ted shouted, 'It's going to be a bastard of a night'—an understatement, as it turned out.

The job in hand was repairs to Polhill Tunnel and the engineers had occupation of the line after the Night Ferry had gone by, at about 9.40, all other traffic being diverted over the Chatham route. We were held at Orpington to let some other trains go by and eventually reached the sidings at Knockholt around 9.15 p.m. Not long to wait. Ted and I finished our first canful of tea and sat eating some of the cakes my mother had made. Ten o'clock; no Night Ferry. Snow was swirling down steadily. 'Must be having a rough trip,' I commented. 'What? Both engines?' said Ted. Very often the Night Ferry would have a Merchant Navy piloted by another engine – an 'L1', a rebuilt Coppertop or something else that Stewarts Lane had handy. Eventually, the Night Ferry went by, unbeknown to us snow in the London area having delayed electric trains. After he had gone, we were signalled out onto the main line and reached the entrance to Polhill Tunnel. Snow was piling up all around and the engineers went ahead of us, their acetylene lamps lighting up the gloom of the tunnel, to carry out their work. We moved slowly along as they worked ahead of us, keeping smoke to the minimum for obvious reasons. All night we kept pulling up, standing an hour or so, pull up, and so on, until it was 7 a.m. and time to pack up. We were then to run to Sevenoaks to refill the tender and open the line for normal traffic. When we emerged from the end of the tunnel, there was snow everywhere. Several feet deep too, the wind blowing from the east and bitter cold. The guard had supplied us with water to make our second brew of tea and Ted, looking at the snow, said, "We better make this last, Mick – that weather looks bad.' It was just about getting light, with the clouds dark above us and it was snowing heavily.

We had already been on duty something like fifteen hours. We made the fire right up to the baffle and the platelayers cleared the snow in the cutting ahead, and having a few minutes break on the footplate in relays to warm-up and rest, then back to work. The snow eased off but not until mid-day did we reach Sevenoaks. The line was blocked from Tonbridge upwards, so our relief had to come from Hither Green. We refilled the tender with water and fortunately had plenty of coal left. There was no turn-table at Sevenoaks so we had to run tender-first back to Knockholt, where we were put into the sidings, as we could not get through to Orpington. We eventually got relieved by a set from Hither Green around seven o'clock Sunday night. My mother had rung Bricklayers Arms and enquired where I was; Jim Foote, I gathered, spoke to her and told her I was out playing trains in Kent and just would not come home! I got a call next morning (Monday) altering my turn of duty from 6.30 to 8.30 a.m., since I had done a bit of extraordinary overtime. However, I came in at eleven-thirty and no one said a word!

Ted and I had many other duties together, but none as arduous as that night at Polhill, though we did hold the record from New Cross Gate to Forest Hill with a goods train and an engine badly in need of visiting the works. This 'record', which earned Ted Biggs the name of 'Brighton Speed King', was one hour fifty minutes for the three-mile journey. . . .

In between duties on the road, time was spent 'in the Yard', where time and again one would hear some tales of personalities long since gone. For instance, one driver had a bad stammer and became known by everyone as 'Machine Gun Dick'. Working the 2.45 a.m. to Gravesend West Street one day, the train ran away with 'M.G.D.' and his fireman, the guard being obviously fast asleep. As the train approached Southfleet station, handbrake hammered hard on and engine in reverse, M.G.D. shouted to his fireman 'I-I-I-I d-d-d-don't th-th-th-think we-we-we can p-p-p-pull up, m-m-m-mate.' They entered Gravesend West Street station much too fast for the fireman's liking; he jumped from the engine and was lucky to get away with bad bruises and a broken leg. The engine ground to a halt at the stops overlooking the River Thames below and knocked one of the buffers from the stops. This went up into the air and straight through the wooden deck of a passing barge! The driver wrote on his report, 'Damage to one ship by loosely fixed buffer'.

Other characters were 'Slim' Roberts, a driver of huge proportions and a driver nicknamed 'Bent Axle' who had a bowed leg! Then there was the tale about 'Polly' Newington, who imitated parrots! One morning, while working the 3.40 a.m. London Bridge to Hastings paper train, Polly and his fireman were more than a little surprised when a man jumped down from the tender of their Schools and landed by their side. Polly, thinking he was a maniac, hit the man one almighty blow on the chin and he was carried from the footplate at Sevenoaks, still 'out'. Evidently this character had climbed along the coach footboards for a bet, then up and over the tender. How he had not been knocked from the train by one of the many overbridges was a mystery. As a postscript, Driver Newington ended his days happily walking around Waterloo station with a dog, collecting money for the Southern Railway Orphanage at Woking.

Bricklayers Arms had a large repair shop and a wheel-turning lathe, where wheels were given a new lease of life. A Merchant Navy, 21C15, was brought in, a Nine Elms engine on loan to Stewarts Lane, which had no wheel turning equipment. The centre driving wheels were dropped and put in the shops for turning, the engine being left outside the adjacent line, called 'the Hay Road'. In front of her was 21C115, a West Country which had had her wheels done and was ready to leave. On a very foggy night – and in those days a very foggy night in London was unbelievably bad for visibility, the foreman told the firelighter to light up No. 21C115. You have already guessed what happened, no doubt – he lit up 21C15. When the crew came to take 21C115 out, they found no fire in her and seeing the Merchant Navy behind them assumed she was to be their engine since smoke was coming from the chimney. The driver, oiling her up by the smoky light of a flare-lamp, called his fireman and said, 'Someone has pinched a pair of me wheels'. Some wit pinned a notice on the engineman's notice board with the caption to a sketch, 'Enginemen are requested to ensure they have a full set of wheels before preparing their engines'. The foreman had a few choice words with the firelighter, who was dubbed some unprintable names.

One afternoon, Ted and I were 'as Required', being given three engines to put away and get ready. One of them, a W.D. 2–8–0, had the longest firebox I had ever seen, and this class took some doing in the hour allowed. We were due off at 1 a.m. and got another W.D. to put away and get ready around 11.30. Ted finished his oiling about 12.30 and managed to get up to London Bridge to catch the last train home. My tram went at 1.10 and I missed it by a couple of minutes; the next one meant an hour to wait. I went into the depot and thought I might have a chat with some of the other 'as Required' men to pass the time. However, the lobby was empty. The foreman that night was Percy Molyneaux, an ex-New Cross man. He came up to me. 'I thought you had finished for the night – are you hungry?' (the term for seeking more overtime).

'No, Perce, that second W.D. you gave us took a bit longer than I bargained for, so I missed my tram home'. Perce pulled a face. 'I haven't got a man in the place and there is a Small Radial to get ready for the 1.45 banker to Forest Hill. If you would get her ready, I will book you an extra hour and a half. How about it?' I agreed, and filled the sands, cleaned and filled the lamps, then made up the fire. Having filled the Donkey and cleaned the cab lights, I left the engine ready and stepped into Perce's office. Driver Hemsley was in there and he and Perce were having a few words. I interrupted. 'She's all ready, Perce!' He thanked me then said, 'Ere! You live at Forest Hill don't you?' I nodded.

Perce grinned at me and Driver Hemsley. 'As you so kindly got me out of a spot of bother getting Driver Hemsley's engine ready, I'm sure he'd be pleased to give you a ride to Forest Hill.' 'Gladly,' answered Driver Hemsley giving me a pleasant smile. I could not understand how they could have been arguing one minute then both smiling the next. But I accepted the offer – I'd already missed the next tram by this time.

Back on the footplate, a very new hand was trying to fire through the tip-flap door. I offered to show him how. We had a chat, then the truth dawned on me. This was the lad's very first firing turn – banking engine from Willow Walk to Forest Hill, the hardest banking duty going. No wonder I had been offered a lift home! Cheeky devils, I thought. Help the foreman out, then end up firing all the way home!

And how I worked going home! Driver Hemsley was determined to give the train engine all the help he could. I was pleased that I had made up a good fire. Jack Glews' advice – 'always prepare an engine as if you are going to run the train yourself', held good once again. I got off at Forest Hill and walked home, thoroughly exhausted, vowing never again to go out of my way to help a foreman out.

A few weeks later, I moved an engine off the coal-stage without making sure the turntable road was clear and collided with another engine. Worse still, we were buffer-locked and were blocking the turntable road. Perce Molyneaux was the foreman on duty. By some expert driving technique, he and the other driver freed the two engines without the assistance of the breakdown gang, who were all for removing the locked buffers. I was angry with myself, and the driver I was fireman to that particular day was not very pleased with me either. After putting the engine away, I went to see Perce to find out when I would have to go before the governor over the accident. Perce looked up from his little desk and grinned at me. 'What accident, son? I ain't seen no accident! Time you went home.' I learned a lesson to keep a sharp lookout and realised that Foreman Molyneaux had not forgotten my helping him out earlier.

It was time to move up a link and Ted Biggs wished me the best of luck. We had got on well and I had learned more from him. Looking at the roster sheet, I found I was booked to be regular fireman to none other than Bert Longhurst. Once again I was fortunate to have another excellent tutor and splendid driver. Our first duty together was a relief turn, the 9.15 a.m. Charing Cross to Dover on a Sunday morning – fast from Waterloo East to Folkestone Central in 83 minutes, with a Spam. I hoped that it would be a good trip; nothing like starting off on the right foot.

CHAPTER FIVE

No. 4 Link

Bert Longhurst was a short tubby man, with a dry Cockney wit. We signed on and after reading the notices, caught a No. 21 bus to London Bridge, then on the train to Charing Cross. He chatted away and was pleased to learn that I had fired a Spam before. It was springtime and the top link crew who would normally have the train were on holiday, whilst the No. 3 men who would normally have covered this turn had a boat train. The engine was Battle of Britain *Spitfire*, later to be tragically involved in the Lewisham accident in 1957.

She dropped back for steam approaching Hither Green and Bert said, 'Sit down Mick, you are working too hard! I've got her notched well up – she'll come round.' By Grove Park, all was well and I had a very pleasant run on Bricklayers Arms' fastest turn at that time. Passing Tonbridge starter I noted the time and I heard a loud chuckle from Bert. 'You've heard of me, no doubt', he said. I soon understood what he meant. He opened the regulator into the second valve, pulled her right up and *Spitfire* was well away. We passed Ashford starter in 19 minutes dead, according to my watch. 'I reckon they will have you for low flying!' I shouted over to Bert.

That first trip with him was to be the fastest time between Tonbridge and Ashford that I ever covered and I reckoned that we did 'the ton' near Headcorn, though bearing in mind our average of 83 m.p.h. and that we had passed Tonbridge at about 45, this would have taken some doing.

One morning, Bert and I were booked a Ramsgate Excursion. Jim Foote was the foreman and he sat back on his rickety chair when I asked him what engine he had for us, Bert being in ear-shot. 'Well now! We have one of Ashford Loco's best, for you and Bert Longhurst – No. 1572. Just right for the Greenwich Line!' The number was not a familiar one and I heard Bert burst out laughing, so I imagined it was an engine with a reputation for poor steaming. It turned out to be a 'C' class but with the help Charlie Dickinson had given me, I knew just what to do. I filled the firebox up with every knob of coal I could find. By the time Bert had read the notices and made his way to the engine, I was throwing coal forward on the tender. Bert opened the firehole doors and smiled. 'Do you reckon we will be able to burn all that in there, Mick?' he enquired. Bert was very light on coal, always notching up early and never seemed to have to hurry in order to keep time.

We picked our empties up from Rotherhithe Road and took them to Deptford, from where the excursion started around 11 a.m., the return fare being about nine shillings and sixpence (47½p)! We stopped at Greenwich, Maze Hill, then Woolwich Arsenal, fast to Dartford, Gravesend and then non-stop to Whitstable, with nine bird-cage coaches. It poured with rain all the way down, but from the engine point of view, we had a lovely trip. I suppose it was around 1.15 when we reached Ramsgate and it was into the depot to put her away, then home pass. I treated Bert to two pints and he asked me who had shown me how to handle a 'C' class in the way I had. I mentioned Charlie Dickinson and Bert nodded his approval. 'Only way to treat a "C", Mick – fill the box up and keep it full'. A few days later Bert told me 'Footie' had enquired how I had got on and was surprised when Bert told him 'Bloomin' lovely, Jim'.

On the back shift the following week, we got the return half of a 'Blackheath' excursion – pass from Victoria down to Ramsgate. We had a look at the train engine; it was a new Spam, named after the chairman of the Southern Railway, *Sir Eustace Missenden.* The Stewards Lane crew eyed us suspiciously, then invited us up in the cab when we said we were from the Brick, pass to Ramsgate. She was brand new and looked very smart. Bert read the nameplate irreverently as 'Sir Useless Missenden' and we got into the train out of the way as a swarm of young trainspotters started asking questions. At Ramsgate loco we had time for our sandwiches and a can of tea, then in to see the foreman. He told us that we had a brand new engine for our excursion back. Bert nodded gravely. 'Sir Eustace Useless, I presume'. The foreman was taken aback. 'How did you know that?' Bert stroked his chin, thoughtfully. 'Had a look over her at the Vic before we had a ride behind her! She'll do, mate'.

We had an uneventful trip back, though I commented to Bert that Ramsgate loco had not been too generous with the amount of coal left in the tender, after we had made up our fire. Passing Rainham, we got checked and Bert mumbled that the signalmen ought to drink tea and not cocoa, then they would be able to keep awake. Gillingham distant, however, remained 'on' despite our repeated whistling—or rather 'hooting'. Five minutes passed and I got down from the footplate, since we had been held at Gillingham outer home for the full five minutes, required me to go to the signalman and remind him of our presence (Rule 55). He told me, after I had signed the Train Register, that an electric train had become derailed in Gillingham station and that the breakdown crew were already at work. 34090 *Sir Eustace* was blowing her head-off and we just had to wait – and wait we did, for one hour and a quarter. By the time we reached Blackheath, the coal supply in the tender was down to a few shovelfuls of dust, but Bert cheerfully accepted this and said, 'We've got her home and the tender is all ready for some decent Bricklayers Arms coal'.

A little while later, Bert had his holiday and a driver by the name of Bob Beaumont took his place. He was known as 'Jammy' Bob, for rumour had it that on his first attempt on the football pools, he won several hundred pounds! On the Saturday, we were pass to Dover, to work an up boat train. Upon arrival, we were given a Bricklayers Arms School, No. 920 *Rugby* and I immediately set to and built up the fire. Bob said he was going to have his sandwiches first, then he would oil up. It was a warm evening and I was really sweating by the time I had made up the fire and thrown some coal forward. Bob climbed up onto the footplate and looked at the fire. 'Have you put any over the front of the box yet?' he asked. I said that I had not. 'Good', he said. 'Leave her as she is – our train is cancelled and we are home pass'. This time, if I had eaten my food when he did, I would have saved myself a lot of work! Bob said, 'Fancy a pint? I've got a terrible thirst thinking of all that hard work you have done!' I began to see why he was nick-named 'Jammy'.

He and I then had another 'brewery' special, for Barclay Perkins whose brewery was on the South Bank of the Thames, close to Cannon Street station which, in the early hours of the morning, used to have a rich, malty aroma drifting from the brewery opposite. We had

920 *Rugby* up from Margate, which seemed to be a popular place for these outings, and arrived five minutes early in London. We took home several bottles of beverage as a memento to this day out. Bob later emigrated to Australia and whilst B.R. lost a very capable driver, one of the Australian railway's gained a very good railwayman. . . .

The summer came and went and Bert said to me one afternoon, 'Seen the new rosters, Mick? You are on the revised lot!' A study of the sheets revealed that with an extra 'As Required' link tacked onto the bottom, my promotion up one link led me from No. 4 to No. 4 link!

My new driver was one Joe Bond, and I was to spend a hilarious four months in his company before he went up into No. 3 link. Joe smoked an evil-smelling Meerschaum pipe. Our first turn of duty was the 1.9 p.m. Vans to Brighton from London Bridge. It was a front shift duty – just – signing on at 11.50 a.m., prepare the engine, then light to London Bridge. We had a Brighton Mogul. 'This job is a New Cross leftover,' said Joe. 'We stop at New Cross Gate, so that the engine can have a look at its old home, pick up some more vans, then right away to East Croydon where, like all good Brighton duties, we take water and get relieved by Brighton men. Then we have a rest while travelling pass to Peckham Rye, sit in the signalbox, then relieve on a goods back to New Cross Gate, back to the Brick, put and prep and that is it!'

By the time we left New Cross Gate, we had a very long train of vans on but the Mogul made light of it. Joe sat on the little seat, puffing at his pipe, while he watched me fire. 'You are not a Brighton bloke, are you Mick?' he enquired. When I answered 'No! Bricklayers Arms,' he nodded. 'Just wondered! One of my previous mates used to swear each time he fired one of these old girls. . . . Oh well! it's time for another charge-up.' I thought from this last comment he wanted me to put another round of coal on the fire, but soon realised that this was Joe's way of saying it was time for him to re-fill his pipe. We sped up Forest Hill bank and as we passed the station, he jerked his pipe in the direction of the town. 'All the toffs live here,' he said. To men who lived in the area around Bricklayers Arms, Forest Hill had a snobbish reputation. I remained silent as Joe went on, 'Driver Weeks – 'e lives here. Old Moores Almanack (a driver with the initial of O. Moore), 'e lives here; "Popeye" Davis as well. All the bloomin' toffs. And me, Joe – I live here!' Not knowing quite what to say, I pulled a face and waited for more. 'There's always the exception to the rule, ain't there now,' he added with a grin. . . .

We stopped at East Croydon and took water, the Brighton men stepping on board. Joe saluted. 'One homesick Mogul! She was most reluctant to leave New Cross yard with what they have tacked on behind us!' he said.

The Brighton driver commented, 'She's a good 'un, this one, mate.' Joe agreed. 'Yes – she'll do half-hour in thirty minutes any day,' this being a usual Bricklayers Arms description of a good engine. It was obvious our Brighton colleagues did not appreciate Joe's humour.

When we reached Peckham Rye, we entered the box there and sat down. Joe asked the signalman, 'How's your mate, then? Back shift?' 'No!' came the reply 'she's on 24 hours.' I wondered just what they were talking about – a female in a signal box? Never been known – not in 1949! Then from a basket under the levers emerged a tortoiseshell cat. 'Hello!' said Joe, tickling its ear. 'Are you going to take over the levers?' The signalman laughed and opened the door for pussy to go out. 'Watch her, Mick,' said Joe and I saw an incredible sight. The cat sat at the bottom of the steps and looked each way. The up signal was off and the down at danger. Pussy remained seated. When the train had gone by, she looked at the signals again. The down signal was now at clear and she remained motionless. Once the train had passed and both signals were at danger, she made her way carefully across the lines and repeated the procedure before returning to the box, apparently reading both signals before attempting to cross the line. I learned that she had had two sets of kittens in the bushes opposite the box and had brought them, one at a time, back to the box in her mouth – but not before both signals were at danger each time. The kittens all became railway cats, keeping the mice population to a reasonable size. Sad to say, pussy was killed one night, some years later when the engineers had possession of the line and a light engine struck her while the signals were being repaired and were consequently at danger. . . .

Later that week, we had 2070, a B4X class which New Cross men called 'Grey Ladies' or 'Grey Backs', since they were turned out in grey paint when the Southern Railway was formed and took over the L.B.S.C.R. Being interested in all types of engines, I told Joe that this 4–4–0 had once done the journey from Victoria to Brighton in just under 49 minutes. Joe replied that he would see what he could do with her. She made heavy weather up Forest Hill bank and he said he did not think he would make an attempt on the record that day! However, as often happens, things said in jest sometimes come partly true. After taking water at East Croydon, we looked in vain for our relief. Joe told the station foreman he would take the train on to its next stop at Redhill, but would need a conductor after that as he did not know the road. Off we went and she ran very well. At Redhill was one passed fireman who said he knew the road to Three Bridges, but not beyond. Joe looked incredulously at the man. 'How far is it from here to Three Bridges?' 'Ten miles', came the reply.

'Blimey,' said Joe sarcastically. 'You sure you can stand up that long?'

Joe, like me, could not understand a Central Section man not knowing the road to Brighton, although one only signed for routes one really knew, so there it was. At Three Bridges, another passed fireman came on board. 'How far you going to conduct me?' said Joe. 'Haywards Heath?' The Three Bridges man looked hurt.

'Oh no, mate, all the way to Brighton!'

'Thank Gawd for that!' said Joe, 'or I shall run out of room writing down all your names on my ticket.' Uphill to Balcombe Tunnel, then down the 1 in 264, Joe opened 2070 out and the old girl really got a move on. 'We are stopping at Haywards Heath,' called out the conductor.

'Whenever you say!' answered Joe as 2070 hammered along.

The low tender of the B4X seemed to allow more coal dust to blow back into the cab, so that the three of us, in spite of repeated waterings of the coal, resembled sweeps. Approaching Patcham, Joe picked up the shovel and pretended to play it like a banjo. The Three Bridges man looked a little surprised. Joe grinned. 'Since we look like Kentucky Minstrels, we might as well play the old banjo,' he said.

The following week we were the 1.40 a.m. Goods to Ramsgate via St. Mary Cray and Chatham, a W.D. duty. These big 2–8–0s were extremely powerful and I doubt if their capacity was ever taxed to the full on the Southern.

A heavy thunderstorm, with torrential rain, was in progress as we set off with 85 and a brake from our first stop at Swanley. On unfitted goods trains it was the fireman's responsibility to exchange hand signals with the guard when passing through a junction and leaving a siding, to ensure the train was complete. The rain was so heavy, it was impossible to see half way down the train, let alone the guard's brake. Off we went. The engine had made easy work of its load from Bricklayers Arms and pulling away from Swanley we soon settled down to the steady clink-clank which easily identified a W.D. Joe opened her out through Farningham and got all the couplings taut as we got to Sole Street summit. Down the bank, the powerful steam brake held the train easily in check, causing Joe to remark, 'You would never think what a load we have on. An 'N' would not like it, Mick.' We pulled up in Chatham and the shunter called out, 'How many, mate?'

'Eighty-five and a brake,' answered Joe.

'You bloody well haven't,' came the reply. The rain was pouring down. 'We bloody well have,' retorted Joe.

'Get your mate to count them, then, driver,' said the sopping wet shunter. Back I went, reluctantly. Sixty-four and no brake was all I could find. The shunter was laughing. 'The guard was asleep when the shunters found him and the rest of the train, still in the siding at Swanley, where you left him!'

Strange as it may seem, we never heard another official word about that incident but we later heard that there were no broken couplings either on our last wagon or the first one of the portion left behind, which seemed to indicate that someone at Swanley had forgotten to re-couple after shunting! I did, however, make sure that the guard and I exchanged handsignals with a white light whenever the visibility allowed.

Three months later, working the same turn, we had a curious experience. We came out of Sorting Sidings and slowly climbed up to join the main line near North Kent East box. We had to stop at the signal at the top of the climb which, when cleared, allowed us onto the main line. We waited a couple of minutes and the signal turned to yellow. Joe opened the regulator but the W.D. refused to budge. He opened the cylinder cocks, to try again. Approaching us was a transfer goods from Hither Green to the L.M.S. Our starter was still showing one yellow and to our amazement the short L.M.S. train crossed over in front of us and carried on towards London Bridge. We still had one yellow. Joe got down and onto the telephone, by which time the signal had gone to red. The signalman assured Joe that the linemen were working on the signals and if we had got one yellow it would only have been momentarily so! Joe made out a report when we returned later that morning to the depot but nothing more was said on the subject. However, we were convinced that we had been given one yellow and had our 2–8–0 pulled away at the first time of asking, a nasty collision would have taken place.

The following week, we had what was known as No. 2 relief week, covering the various front shift 'day off' or 'rest day' duties; I cannot remember the exact order, but the duties are still very clear. The hardest one was the 4.50 'Old Road' newspaper train to Margate, via Redhill and Tonbridge, signing on at 2.30 a.m., engine all ready. 2.45 light to Rotherhithe Road and take the 3.8 a.m. empties to Cannon Street, then light to London Bridge and back onto the train. Make up the fire, throw every bit of coal well forward, breakfast (fried egg, bacon and fried bread) on the shovel and off at 4.50, first stop East Croydon, arrive 5.7, depart 5.10, then Purley, Coulsdon South, Merstham and Redhill, arrive 5.36, depart at 5.51. The long wait at Redhill was due to the large amount of mail transferred from the main sorting office there. Miss Nutfield, call at Godstone, Edenbridge, Penshurst, Lyghe Halt and Tonbridge, arriving there at 6.27, taking water and throwing more coal forward. Off again at 6.33, call all stations to Ashford, which was reached at 7.31. We had one hour there and back with the 7.3 a.m. ex-Margate via Canterbury West, which arrived at Ashford at 8.28 and away at 8.30; miss Pluckley, call at Headcorn, Staplehurst, Marden, Paddock Wood and Tonbridge, Hildenborough, Sevenoaks and Knockholt at 9.48, then fast to London Bridge, where we were relieved (if we were lucky) at 10.9.

The next morning we would be down with the Tattenham Goods, and then the next morning down with the 5.8 a.m. London Bridge to Brighton, first stop Peckham Rye, then East Dulwich (omit North Dulwich), Tulse Hill, Streatham, Mitcham Junction, Hackbridge, Carshalton, Sutton, Cheam (omit Ewell East), Epsom (omit Ashtead), Leatherhead (omit Boxhill), and reach Dorking North, twenty-five and a half miles from London Bridge, at 6.30! Then Lomwood, Ockley, Warnham and arrive at Horsham at 7.2, where the public timetable stated that the train terminated. However, at 7.16, off we went again, calling at Christ's Hospital, Southwater, West Grinstead, Partridge Green, Henfield, Steyning, Bramber, Shoreham-by-Sea (omit Southwick), Portslade, Hove and finally – with great relief – into Brighton at 8.24, three hours and sixteen minutes from London Bridge – all this with a 'U' boat! In the winter, it was home pass unless there was an engine out of Brighton Works which needed returning to London, then we took it back.

The next week, something quite different for No. 4 link – the same job all the week. On at 3 p.m. pass to Waterloo and relieve on the 12.36 ex-Margate to Charing Cross. Work the train into Charing Cross, then take the empties round to Cannon Street to form the 4.32 to Ramsgate. Light to Ewer Street, clean the fire and make it up, take coal and water, ready to be relieved by Ashford men at 6.30, who took the engine to Charing Cross to run the 7.15 p.m. down. We had twenty minutes break, then relieved on a 'C' class and ran light to Bexleyheath, where

Brighton K class Mogul No. 2343 photographed 'at home' at New Cross shed.

Schools class 30923 'Bradfield', on which I made my debut on the well-known 6.18 Cannon Street – Dover.

The original Bulleid Pacifics had a smoke problem . . .
[R.H.N. Hardy]

No. 3477, as yet un-named, outside Brighton Works, brand-new.

we did some shunting before running a short goods train back to Bricklayers Arms. Joe used to let me drive down to Bexleyheath and do a bit of shunting.

Saturday evenings in the yard very often consisted of preparing engines for their 'Shed day' when boilers were washed out and of course this meant that all the fire had to be thrown out. The engines were then termed 'dead' and were left in the Carriage Shed, for the boilerwashers' attention. It was the job of the Shed Pilot to move about the engines that were dead. One Saturday night we had just finished duty; it was around 7.30 p.m. and pouring with rain. Joe suggested that we walked through the Carriage Shed, which would keep some of the rain off us. At the end of one of the roads, a gang of cleaners were giving an 'L1' an enthusiastic clean. The senior hand was in the middle of the motions and the gang were singing in unison their own version of 'Give me five minutes more'. We stopped. 'Nice to see a keen, happy cleaning gang', Joe called out to the senior hand. 'The foreman said we can finish as soon as we get her nice and clean', came the reply. Being propelled into the shed, onto the same road as the 'L1', were three dead engines, a Schools and two King Arthurs, in charge of a Brighton Rooter. Joe looked at the slowly approaching engines. 'With this rain, that little Rooter will not stop that lot easily – they will pull her along! Lads, get out from that engine, quickly. Do as I say!' The cleaners scrambled from the engine, Joe and I helping the senior hand out of the motions. We heard the Westinghouse brake applied on the Rooter, and sure enough, the three large engines dragged the tank along. The driver realised what was happening since his fireman had seen the 'Not To Be Moved' sign exhibited on the 'L1'. They reversed the Rooter but the buffers of the School just touched the 'L1'. Had the cleaners remained on her, the senior hand in the motions would certainly have been killed or injured badly. The Rooter driver was white with fear as he thought the cleaners were still on the 'L1'. . . .

We were working the 8.25 a.m. Charing Cross to Hastings one morning, and were running downhill through Hildenborough. Joe called me over to his side and shouted, 'If you were in charge of a train, going at this speed, and had reason to believe that a pair of the driving wheels were off the road, how would you stop?' I realised that to apply the vacuum brake would apply the engine brakes as well as that of the train, and could cause the engine to overturn, but I had never thought of the correct procedure. The answer was to pull the trigger under the brake valve, thereby applying the brakes only to the train and not to the locomotive, with the brake handle left strictly in the running position. This useful tip is stressed by present-day locomotive inspectors to steam crews on preserved lines.

For ten days, Joe went on holiday, and I was paired with an ex-New Cross driver, Fred Belton, who shared my hobby of outdoor model railways. Our first week was a former New Cross duty, and we had an hour to spare in the sidings close to the Cold Blow Signal Works. I was shown what looked like ships' wheels, but was told that they were used to adjust the Whitworth Patent signals which contributed to the Clayton Tunnel accident of 1861! Brighton signals were wooden, slightly wider at one end than the other, with the home signals painted that wonderful 'red with a tinge of carmine' – almost a pinkish hue – which distinguished them from all other company signals. When his father had been at New Cross, Fred Belton told me condemned engines were carefully cleaned and carried a black crepe sash around one buffer before making their way to Brighton Works to be cut-up. This quaint custom underlined the affection which regular crews had for their 'own' engines.

The Running Foremen, as I have already mentioned, sat in a small office overlooking the coal road and could see all engines entering or leaving the depot. As one took its place on the coal road, the driver would report to the foreman and enquire if she was to be put away, got ready for duty number . . . and which road in which shed she was to be stabled. Having given his instructions, the foreman would write down the engine number on a sheet of paper with a cross above the number if she was put away or two crosses if got ready, so at a glance he could see the state of his stud at any given moment. Underneath the engine number he would write the next duty allocated. When the crew signed on, and were allocated an engine, he would draw a line through the number and when he saw it leave the depot, he drew another line through it making a cross. Naturally, the shed and road number where the engine was stabled were put under one of three headings; Old Shed, Carriage Shed or New Shed. A pencil and eraser were all the visible tools a foreman had. Everything else, such as duty numbers, which class each duty required, was carried in his head. Foremen were all ex-drivers and no engineman envied their position one bit. Discipline was easy for footplate staff; very much a question of give-and-take. For instance, when I was 2.30 a.m. on, 2.45 away, the all night tram arrived at the Brick just after 2.30, and by the time I had walked from the Swan Gate to the Foreman's Office, it was gone 2.35. The foremen allowed for this, though of course they could have insisted on a prompt arrival, which would have meant my getting up an hour earlier. By the same token, if I was due to finish in an hour and the foreman was short-handed, needing an engine put away and got-ready (two-hour job), I helped him out. By such means did the locomotive department run.

I have outlined how relieving crews would bring details of the Alteration Sheet with them to avoid having to return to the depot when relieved in London. Sometimes, however, the List Clerk received urgent new engine workings after he had pinned up his list. Men who had to be given new duties were advised by cleaners delivering a call note to their homes. One rarely saw 'the Governor', one Harry Packham. Men 'on the carpet', usually for consistent lateness, had to see Dudley Miles, the Chief Clerk. He dressed in city style, with black pin-striped suit and a bowler, stiff white collar and black tie. A man who had to go up and see him would refer to this as 'going up to see the undertaker'.

General discipline was handled by George Clark. If you missed your turn of duty ('I did not hear the alarm clock, George!') he would say, 'Go and see if the Running Foreman can find you a job. If not bugger off home and be sure to be on time tomorrow!' The Running Foreman was always glad of a spare fireman. If you failed to report for duty, you had to come in to see George Clark before 4 p.m., or else your turn was covered for the next day on the assumption you were sick. It was strictly a case of 'No work – No pay' even if a doctor's certificate was provided.

Discipline on the road was in the driver's hands. If a driver told you to do something, you did it immediately and asked questions afterwards – you learned that on your first day's work as a cleaner. Rarely did a driver report a fireman to the foreman.

In my time there was always a shortage of engine tools and lamps. One could clean and fill the three headlamps necessary on a locomotive, put them on the footplate ready to put in position, and when you turned round, they had gone! It was the same with the long-handled 'scoops' with which the fires were cleaned. Put a scoop down by the side of your engine and take your eyes from it for a while and it, too, vanished. Many of us used to put the handles of scoops into the fire for a few moments to heat up; and sometimes a loud yell would announce that the would-be thief was being deterred from removing someone else's equipment!

On the road, coming up, firing used to finish at Knockholt (unless one was having a rough trip) and the hydrostatic lubricator on a

Schools would be switched off at Hither Green, so as to be nice and cool and easy to refill if the engine was going into Ewer Street for a quick 'put and prep'. Any defect on the engine was reported to the relieving driver upon arrival in London. A fitter could reach Ewer Street from the Brick in half-an-hour. On West Country class locos, the trimmings would be taken out of the oil boxes on the footplate passing Hither Green, the 'oil bath' level being checked daily by the fitting staff before the engine left its home depot.

It was, all too soon, time for Joe to go up into the next link and my new driver was Joe Simmonds. I met him as I signed on. He carried an extra pair of overalls with him. These he put on over his clean overalls while he was oiling up, leaving one set clean and fresh to drive in. He was meticulous in his engine preparation, examining, tapping and double-checking. Joe left nothing to chance and climbed onto the tender for our first trips together to ensure that I had firmly stacked the coal. He had a driving style all of his own and used to rest his elbows on the reversing wheel, standing first on one foot, then on the other, completely relaxed, a hand-rolled cigarette in the corner of his mouth.

Coming up on the 8.30 from Ashford, Joe always reckoned to use the 'blow-down' apparatus which discharged steam, water and sediment, in that order, and reduced shed time for the Spams, after leaving Ashford. I opened the wheels and put on one injector and after the seven seconds of blowing-down had elapsed, turned the wheel to close the valve. On this occasion it broke off, the valve still in the open position. We managed, by using a spanner and some coins, to grip the four-sided spindle, but nearly lost our water. Passing through a station, we sprayed everyone in sight with steam, water and dirt before we managed to close the valve.

We had the same turn three months later and, as usual, when the train ran in, Joe asked the crew if they had filled up with water at Canterbury. They assured us that they had. The engine, 34077 *603 Squadron*, was equipped with a 4,500-gallon tender which was insufficient to do the 100-mile journey. The Pacific was in fine fettle and we had an easy run up. As was the custom, I had finished firing at Knockholt and steam pressure had fallen to 220. No matter, downhill all the way now and with a quarter of a gauge-glass full of water, we had plenty of room to put more water in, to keep her from blowing-off when she came round. There were no dampers on these engines as originally built, so one could not cool down the fire by stopping draught from 'fanning' the fire. Joe had a quick wash in the bucket while I sat on the driver's side and watched the road ahead. Approaching Chislehurst, I put on the injector, since pressure had already passed the 270 mark. By Grove Park, pressure was back to 250. 'That will keep her quiet, Joe!' I shouted, when suddenly, from beneath the engine came a dull roar – the injector had blown-off. Joe commented, 'It's overheating. Put the other one on, Mick'. I opened the water valve and looked through the inspection hole. The reason the first injector had blown-off was all too apparent – there was no water coming out of the pipe! The tender was empty! Joe, cool as a cucumber, looked at the gauge glass – half full. 'If we don't get held up Mick, we'll be alright'. The damperless engine was again making steam and I got the scoop from the tender and made a hole in the fire – bad practice, but the only way to cool her down. Hither Green distant was at caution. That was all we needed! Joe hung on the whistle chain and mercifully the distant came off. Joe put on steam to reduce the pressure and avoid 34077 blowing off and wasting what was now our most precious commodity – water. One blow-off from the safety valves and an inch of water was gone. We got one more signal check, but amid the mass of e.m.u. rush-hour traffic into London, this was not surprising. In spite of all our efforts, the valves lifted again on 34077 as we entered London Bridge station, where our relief was waiting. Joe explained the situation to them and remained at the regulator. The water stood two inches in the glass and from No. 7 Platform it was slightly uphill, indicating we had very little water indeed left in the boiler. We approached Borough Market Junction, a usual place to be held up – one more blow-off and 34077 would be a failure of the worst kind. The four of us were sweating with anxiety. Luck was with us, clear road into Cannon Street. Joe brought her in slowly, braking gently so as not to surge the water away from the crown of the firebox and melt the fusible plugs. I was already up on the tender, lid open – the relief fireman jumped off the engine as we slowly went by the water crane and stood ready to turn it on the moment I got the pipe into the tank hole. As 34077 stopped, the pipe was in and the water gushed into the dry tender. Bill Collins got one injector on, then the second. The water was out of sight in the glass – and on a Spam, which had no bottom nut fitting, that was dangerously low! We all breathed a sigh of relief as the water in the gauge glass began to come into view. Joe lit a cigarette and commented on the parentage of the crew who had assured us that they had filled up at Canterbury. We always personally checked the water supply after that little incident. . . .

Two weeks later, I was Rest Day working and had the 1.9 Vans with a passed fireman, an ex-New Cross man named Stennett. Instead of the usual 'U-Boat', we had a West Country, 34038 *Lynton*, 'on loan' to Brighton. I made up my customary big fire and trimmed the coal. After we had stopped at New Cross Gate, Stennett came over my side and picked up the shovel. 'Never fired one of these,' he said and added, 'You take her down. Stop at East Croydon.' I needed no second bidding, opened out 34038 and we sailed up Forest Hill bank, my mate firing for all he was worth until we reached Forest Hill. *Lynton* maintained 265/270 all the way up the bank and we went through Sydenham with 140 in the steam chest. Needless to say, she was blowing her head off when we stopped at East Croydon. Knowing my driver was a Brighton man, I stopped right for water and he was pleased at that. We filled up the tender and were relieved by Brighton men, before making our way to Peckham Rye and 'pussy-in-the-signalbox' once more.

It was now time to leave Bricklayers Arms and do my eighteen months of military service which, due to the trouble in Korea, extended to two years. I was to find many changes when I returned. . . .

CHAPTER SIX

Back from the Army

FIREMEN RETURNING from National Service were catered for by a short but very helpful familiarisation course, lasting two days, after the usual medical and eye-sight tests. A lot of changes had taken place, with three new designs to deal with. The first day of the course took place underneath Waterloo station, where a well-equipped cinema showed films about safety and what could happen when rules were broken. An Inspector read rules from the Rule Book, one by one and each was illustrated by a short piece of film which vividly brought the particular circumstances to life. A 'quiz' followed, with two teams of firemen competing without reference to the Rule Book – the 1950 B.R. edition having superseded my old Southern Railway one.

Tuesday morning, I went pass to Chislehurst where, in the waiting rooms on the main line platforms (never used), a training school had been set up. In charge was ex-driver F. Brown, from Bricklayers Arms, now an Inspector. Using a model railway, various types of derailments (run-offs) were demonstrated and the method of protection by the placing of detonators. My third day back on the railway was 'as required', cleaning out smoke-boxes, ashpans and cleaning fires; back to the old routine! Next I was booked the 4.50 Old Road down and had Charlie Hayward, who was just finishing his time in No. 1 link. All went well until we entered Bletchingley Tunnel where, half-way through, some joker pulled the communication cord. Contrary to the screaming of swiftly-applied brakes, with all the passengers being thrown to the floor as depicted on the movies, 934 *St. Lawrence* began to drag her feet and Charlie blew the brake off with the large ejector ('shoving the 'andle right up' was the correct term) and managed to get us out of the tunnel. The culprit, we found, was an R.A.F. man who had boarded the wrong train at Redhill!

My next turn was a troop special to Folkestone, the engine of which had a very small fire in it. Being a Spam, it refused to steam and we had to fight to get by Bridge 179. The next day, I was booked with my old New Cross friend, Fred Belton, who casually commented in passing he had not seen me around lately. When I told him I had been two years in the army, he found it hard to believe.

Our job was to take an 'L1' to New Cross Gate and take twelve coaches to Lancing Works for overhaul. No. 31788 did not like climbing Forest Hill bank with twelve on from a cold start at New Cross Gate and we took eleven minutes from starting to pass Forest Hill. Then up over the Quarry – another long climb, though not so steep; Lancing at last, light to Brighton and put her away. By then I knew by my aching back that I had done a good day's work.

We rode back in the cab of a 6-Pul/6-Pan e.m.u. to Victoria, and I had to go on the handle for about twenty miles. We returned to the Brick where I found my name was not on the Alteration Sheet. At first, I thought they had given me the day off but no, I was up in No. 2 link, with Tom Merrett, another ex-New Cross man. Fred said. 'You've got one of our best drivers, Mick,' and he was right. Our first job together was the dreaded 6.18 out of Cannon Street. Tom was taller than me, with black eyebrows that gave him the appearance of a permanent frown. Tom's previous fireman was one Perce Chopping, and I knew I would have to work very hard to come up to Chopping's standard. According to Fred Belton, he could make any engine blow off steam, no matter how hard she was being worked; he was a man of great strength and could even straighten the long poker, called a 'dart', across his chest – and a dart was one-inch diameter iron!

I signed on a bit early and got up to Cannon Street, eager to get onto the footplate and look at the fire. I need not have worried. Sitting on the driver's seat was Jack Glew, smiling away, who greeted me with the kind remark, 'Blimey! They must be hard up in No. 2 gang – they have taken old Mick!' He looked at the fire and tapped the side of the cab. 'I expect you remember this old girl, 923 *Bradfield*?' I most certainly did, for our first job together back in 1948 had been on this very

L1 31757 – a good performer on a Race Special to Westenhanger in 1948.

No. 2590 was the E5 Radial tank with which we – almost – banked 'the Hornby'.

C Class 1711: 'an Ashford engine, working home on a Hopper via the main line'.

train. Tom Merrett came up onto the footplate and Jack got off the seat. 'What have you done with Perce then, Tom? Killed him?' Tom shook his head and grinned. 'He says he's going to work on some real fast trains!' he said. I thought it was time to introduce myself and interrupted them. 'Mike Jackman – just out of the army,' I said, looking up at Tom and wondering how good he had thought Perce Chopping. 'Hurrah for the bloomin' Life Guards,' he said jovially. 'Ordnance,' I answered, getting the reply, 'Never heard of 'em! But put it there, mate!' We shook hands.

Jack told me that while I was taking life easy in the army, poor Joe Simmonds had been catapulted across the footplate of his engine when it was struck by a runaway and badly hurt. I was very sorry to hear that as Joe was such a conscientious man and it was so unfair for someone else's negligence to injure him.

Tom looked at his watch. 'The customers will be expecting us to get a move on in a minute, Jack,' he said, whereupon Jack and his mate left the footplate. Tom pointed to the next road, where a West Country, blowing off furiously, was about to depart. 'That,' said Tom, 'is the blighter we have got to beat getting by Chislehurst station! He leaves at 6.16, goes down the slow road (No. 2) through London Bridge – we go down No. 3 road – they take bloomin' bets, the regular travellers do, as to which engine gets first at the country end of Chislehurst'. As Tom finished speaking, a 'regular' approached the cab. Tom leaned down to listen, as I put the injector on, to keep 923 quiet.

'Are we going to be first, tonight, driver?' the man enquired. 'We'll do our best, guv', we'll do our best!'

'Good man!' came the reply. 'We have a few pounds on you!'

The man returned to his carriage. Tom looked at the fire and returned to his side of the footplate. Doors slammed shut, a shrill blast on the guard's whistle and the green flag. On the adjacent road, the 6.16 had rounded Borough Market Junction and the Ramsgate driver had to keep his train in check through the 15 m.p.h. limit through No. 2 platform at London Bridge. Tom opened the regulator fully into the first valve. *Bradfield* moved slowly away, without a trace of a slip. I sounded the whistle. Tom was leaning out of the cab and I joined him to get a view of Borough Market signals. 'Two yellows – that will get us into London Bridge! Tom said. He gave the regulator a cuff and '923' responded like the lady she was. I picked up the shovel; Jack Glews' fire was bright yellow already and in went the first seven shovelfuls. On with the injector, a quick glance at the lubricator – yes, that was working okay, now what had we got ahead? I leaned out as we entered the right-hand curve outside London Bridge, a pall of smoke from the 6.16 covering the signals, but the colour light shone through it. I held out my left hand, palm open, 'Green 3, Tom'.

'Hold on to your hats, here we come', said Tom and 923 went into the second valve. The noise of the coupling and connecting rods was clearly audible as we steamed through London Bridge. I fired again, pressure hovering on 215; I wanted that extra five pounds. The 6.16 was passing Peak Freans – maybe a thousand yards ahead. Another seven shovelfuls as we overhauled an electric on the Central Section, the passengers jammed packed. I looked at the pressure gauge – just 220. I shouted to Tom, 'You can give her a bit more, mate.' Tom moved the reverser forward from 25 to 30 per cent. and one could feel *'Bradfield'* increase her stride. Another round. North Kent East, right hand curve now – New Cross ahead, partly obscured by the smoke from the Spam on the 6.16. 'Green', I called. Tom nodded and I crossed to his side to get a view of the 6.16. 'I reckon we are gaining on him', I shouted above the roar of the exhaust. Through Tanners Hill, into the cutting; Tom could see the signals now, so on with another round. St. Johns. 'Green', I shouted and hung on to the grab rail as we made the sharp right hand bend. The fire was perfect and she was holding on 220, the injector singing away. The uphill climb had begun. Although a Brighton man, Tom handled a School as well as any South Eastern driver. He increased the cut-off a bit more on the 1 in 140 and shouted to ask how I was doing. I pointed to the gauge, stock still on 220; Tom opened the regulator a bit more. The rear of the 6.16 was only a couple of hundred yards away now. As the gradient steepened to 1 in 120, Tom left the engine alone. He was not going to press her too much. Two miles to Elmstead Woods and 923 dropped back slightly to 210; I shut off the injector and gave her another seven. Tom opened the regulator fully into the second valve. The noise was exciting, even though some of my fire was coming out of the chimney. *Bradfield* was back on 220 and on went the injector before I fired again. We were now level with the last coach on the 6.16. I shut off the injector and pointed to the reverser. 'Go on, Tom! Give her a bit more – she'll take it!' Tom moved the reverser another 5. I fired again; still 220. 'Five more coaches and we will be level,' he yelled. I came over to his side. Four, three, two. Passengers in the 6-16 were nodding and making gestures to their opposite numbers in our train and a few fists were shaken at us as we slowly overhauled the Spam. Tom got hold of the whistle chain and gave him a blast. The fireman was too busy to notice us but the driver opened out the Pacific. From Chislehurst Tunnel we burst out with the Spam almost level. Tom moved the lever forward, for our clear road ahead. We had done it, but only just. The Spam hooted at us as he took the gentle left hand turn-off and I put the injector on and fired again. 'That will show the tin-lizzie Bulleid bloomin' wonder!' said Tom.

We made the stop at Sevenoaks and two city gents came up. 'Splendid! driver, absolutely splendid! You and your fireman have a drink on us," and he handed Tom two ten-shilling notes. While taking water at Tonbridge, we were handed two half-crowns and then another five shillings when we reached Ashford. . . .

We adjourned to The Kent Arms just outside Ashford station, well pleased with our first trip together. I must add that we did not catch the 6.16 the rest of the week, however, for the Ramsgate driver drove the Spam mercilessly, until Friday, when his charge primed badly near Grove Park and we thereupon passed him easily.

A week later, we were booked the 5.8 a.m. London Bridge to Brighton. As we booked on, Jim Foote, the foreman, came out to see us. 'Bad news for you two I'm afraid. Norwood men with their new diesel have pinched your job, so go and sit in the lobby.' What a nerve – two No. 2 link men 'as required'! Tom and I put an Arthur away and got a School ready. The next morning, the same thing – Norwood were going to run the 5.8. Tom had a good moan. 'Forty-four years on the footplate and still doing boys' work!' Jim Foote nodded in sympathy. At that moment, the telephone rang and the message was that the Norwood diesel had failed at London Bridge – could an engine get up there quickly? Tom came joyfully to life. 'Right then, Jim, where's our trusty steed?' '42104', came the quick reply.

'Blimey! What's that, Tom?'

'They call them 'Midlands'. I'd have more confidence in an 13!' said Tom. Remembering my couple of trips up Freshfield bank between Sheffield Park and Horsted Keynes with an ageing 13, I did not feel confident in making the acquaintance of the L.M.R. 2–6–4 tank. Still, no time to ponder, the 5.8 was waiting for an engine, since the diesel had failed.

I had to make up the fire as we ran light to London Bridge, one which suited the sloping firebox of the engine. The 5.8 only consisted of six coaches and we arrived at London Bridge at five past five – three minutes to couple up, make a brake test and be away. With our first stop at Peckham Rye, the Midland kept her steam, the run was uneventful and I said something to the effect that she was not a bad engine – for a Midlander. Tom's reply, however, set me thinking.

'Wait until you get the 4.20 down next week – nine on and nine minutes to pass Forest Hill – then tell me what you think of them!' The next week, back shift, we were 3.15 on, 3.30 away, light to London Bridge with 42108, another 'Midland' 2–6–4T. She was 'seen away', and the preparation crew had made up a lovely fire, the coal being Yorkshire Hards – the fireman's friend. Tom told me that we had a race with an electric which was non-stop between London Bridge and Norwood Junction; it left the Bridge two minutes after we did. 'Right away' and with a sharp bark the 2–6–4T pulled smartly away, with full regulator in the first valve and the cut-off set at 50 per cent. Steam dropped from 200 to 190 and the injector had not been put on – a promising start. Firing steadily, I got pressure up to 200, but the water was half way down the gauge glass; on with the injector. By Bricklayers Arms Junction, we must have been doing 50 m.p.h. and the tank was rolling a bit; Tom had wound her back to 40 per cent and I increased my rate of firing. We whistled, as was the custom, as we tore through New Cross Gate and started to climb Forest Hill bank. Pressure had dropped to 190, but we still only had 'half-a-glass' so the injector had to remain on. I built the fire up right up to the baffle plate whereupon, lo-and-behold, the pressure started to rise. Tom opened the regulator into the second valve and this stopped her blowing off. He looked behind as we neared Brockley. 'Here comes the bloomin' juice train.' I went over and had a look. An eight-car train of two 4-SUB units was half a mile behind. Back to the firing, three-quarters of a glass of water, 195 on the clock. Another round. Tom shouted out, 'The blighter is ruddy well jet propelled!' I shut the injector off and pressure touched 200. 'Give her the gun, Tom,' I said, and Tom did. The Midlands had self-cleaning smokeboxes, which simply meant that the ash was ejected out with the exhaust and not left to lie in the foot of the smokebox. 42108 was certainly emptying her smokebox as we passed Forest Hill in 9½ minutes – half-a-minute down in spite of our hurrying! Once over the top we galloped down through Sydenham, still on full regulator, but notched up to around 25 per cent. The engine was wallowing about and Tom eased the regulator into first valve. Injector on, water in the bottom of the glass but 195 still on the clock. A shrill whistle alongside announced the electric had levelled with us. The motorman grinned across at us, and Tom opened up 42108 into full regulator. The former would have the handle right round in parallel but we knew he would soon have to shut off ready to slow down for his stop at Norwood Junction. We saw him shove the handle back to off and we left him slowly behind. According to Tom's watch, we were 'on time' at East Croydon, having regained that lost half-a-minute. A minute's stop there and off we went, next stop Oxted. Seventeen minutes were allowed for this section and we needed every one. We arrived at East Grinstead at 5.19 and took water and a short rest of sixteen minutes. I broke up more coal in the bunker, remade the fire while Tom went to the porters' room to make a can of tea. Onto Sheffield Park, where we had seven minutes and left the staff for the single line and rejoined the double track, into Lewes and finally arrived at Brighton at 6.46.

Incidentally, the Norwood diesel, No. 10800, was known by steam enginemen on the Central Section as the 'Wonder Engine'—from the Locomotive Department's daily query, 'I wonder if it will go today?'

Our return trip was with the 8.19 from Lewes, travelling via Sheffield Park, East Grinstead and Oxted to arrive in London Bridge at 10.17 p.m. Tom asked me to count the number of passengers that got on and off and by the end of the week (the duty ran on Saturday night as well) we averaged ten passengers in the train per night! On the return trip I made the acquaintance of the Class 2MT Ivatt 2–6–2 tank (41316) which had a tremendous turn of speed. Tom, like most Southern enginemen, called them 'Teddy Bears' and they became great favourites. The next night going down, we had a Standard Class 4, built at Brighton and numbered in the 80 000 series, which gave rise to their unofficial classification of the 80 000 Class. However, as for most things on the railway, there was a more descriptive nick-name and due to the fact that the reversing wheel was edge-on to the reversing shaft, the handle reminded men of the handle of a bacon-slicing machine on a grocery counter, so the Standard Class 4 became known as the 'Bacon Slicers'.

On my first trip, I found it hard to keep at the full working pressure of 225 psi but, as experience grew, this was achieved; however, they somehow did not have the power you could get out of a 'Midland'. Nevertheless, they were comfortable engines to work on, being easy to dispose of and get ready, as everything was 'get-attable'. They were equipped with speedometers and of course, no fireman could resist the temptation of covering this and then asking the driver to estimate his speed. Seldom was a driver's estimate of speed more than 5 m.p.h. out!

The regulator of a 'Bacon Slicer' had to be left open when making a stop, in order for the throttle-controlled lubricator to supply oil to the cylinders. A coloured gauge on the driver's side had a red section, which the needle should not enter whilst the locomotive was in motion, to remind the driver to keep the regulator slightly open when making a stop. Tom commented that this 'wonderful invention' must cause more wear on the brake blocks and use more coal and water when compared to the 'old-fashioned' engines.

The Rest Day arrangements did not always guarantee a regular crew working together and one back shift Rest Day working sent Tom piloting one of our drivers down to Brighton via Oxted, and myself pass to Gravesend. Needless to say, I rode down from Dartford to Gravesend Central. My driver on this occasion was Charlie Ranger, who rode down in the cab with me.

Our job, however, was not on the Gravesend line itself, but on the little-used branch known as the Gravesend West Street line. This was completed in 1886, to coincide with the opening of the pier. The line was the property of the London, Chatham & Dover Railway and was an attempt to rob the South Eastern of passengers for Gravesend and because the Gravesend Central station was very short of space, all goods traffic centred on the West station, which had a large goods yard. The branch left the old Chatham line at Fawkham Junction, though for ease of train working the 'branch' was deemed to extend from Farningham Road station, a distance of six miles 1,466 yards between signal-boxes. The ruling gradient was 1 in 100 uphill from Gravesend West. In 1952, when the passenger service still ran (five each way Monday to Friday, eight up and seven down on Saturdays, no service on Sundays) there were three stations en route – Rosherville Halt, Southfleet Station, and Longfield Halt. Sidings built to serve British Portland Cement, named Perry Street sidings, left the line from Rosherville (350 yards from the halt on the London side), with a fork serving Bowater's Paper Mills. Passenger traffic was withdrawn in 1953. As Charlie Ranger told me, this little branch used to carry boat trains from Victoria for the Batavia Line steamers to Rotterdam. These trains were unique for they called at Bromley South and at Longfield Halt on the way down! They were withdrawn at the outbreak of World War II, the traffic being transferred to the St. Pancras – Tilbury route, never to return.

We did some shunting and made up our train of some fifteen wagons and a brake, and followed the 'H' class passenger train consisting of a two-coach pull and push set. We left West Street at 8.30, stopped in Hither Green and got into Bricklayers Arms at 11.50 p.m. – a very interesting day out into railway history.

Tom and I worked through the rosters and on our next Rest Day working we were paired together on a Ramsgate – Victoria relief train. Our engine was 34065 *Hurricane* and Tom showed me how she could climb the dreaded Sole Street Bank. We reached 'the Vic' and were due to be relieved by Stewarts Lane men but, as was often the case in the summer, no relief was available, so it was light to Stewarts Lane or, as Tom still insisted on calling it, 'Battersea', after the old Brighton depot there (which amalgamated with the old 'Chatham' depot of Longhedge and became known as Stewarts Lane). I had to go and see the foreman to see if we were to be relieved. The foreman that evening was none other than Fred Pankhurst, late of our own depot. His familiar steel-rimmed spectacles glinted in the evening sun as he screwed up his face and recognised me, although it was over two years since I had last seen him. 'Watch your pockets! Here's a Bricklayers Arms man!' was the greeting I received. We chatted for a minute and before I knew what I was doing, he persuaded me to put *Hurricane* away for him, although all Tom had to do was take out the trimmings on the footplate.

Fred was a great character, whose photographic memory for faces and duties was known throughout the South Eastern section. His management of men would be a lesson to some of today's 'executives' and his ability to get things done by talking men into 'helping him out' was an example of what is termed today 'man management ability'.

While I cleaned the fire, Tom sat on the driver's seat and seemed amused that I had 'volunteered' to put a Battle of Britain away after a day's work on the road. I told Tom that if 'Pankie' came and asked us to get her ready, he would most likely succeed. Tom scoffed at the very idea but I am sure old Pankie would have convinced Tom – and I – that he had not got another man in the place to do it.

Tom let me have the regulator coming up from Brighton one morning, with a Teddy Bear on 'the Birkenhead' and I did not touch the fire from Brighton to Redhill, where we came off. It seems as if the method of 'knobbing-up' was not the sole property of Charlie Dickinson, since Tom recalled how on the Brighton Fasts (the term Express was never used on the Brighton) he used to make up the fire on an Atlantic at Brighton and run up to London without firing. He treated our Teddy Bear the same way and I thoroughly enjoyed being driver.

Our last week together was with the 7.34 Charing Cross to Dover, coming off at Ashford and returning with the 11 p.m. Goods, fast to Paddock Wood and the Brick. This fast freight running was the reason that the 'N' class were introduced and they did the job superbly. Fire made up at Ashford, Tom sat on the fireman's seat and I ran the train. The regulator open a mere 'crack', notched well up, we kept up a steady 45 m.p.h. to Paddock Wood. Drop off a few, pick up a few, make up the fire and off again homewards.

At the end of that memorable week, having got in some 300 miles driving, Tom and I looked at the 'Sheet' and found that he was promoted into No. 1 link. My new driver was William T. Snell, another tremendous character, but as he had another week's holiday to finish, I had a different driver each day, which made life very interesting. The following week, we were pass to Cannon Street, for the famous 6.18 down.

We set off for Ashford and Bill watched the fire being thrown by the Spam on the 6.16 running ahead of us. He had seated himself on the small tip-up seat of our Schools and we set off in pursuit of the Spam, using half regulator and a cut-off of 30 per cent, which remained unchanged until Knockholt. Even so, the 6.16 only just beat us to Chislehurst and Bill did not resort to knocking my fire about. The week ended after three wins for the 6.16 plus one tie and one victory for us.

A couple of weeks later, we had a 'down, round and back turn'; take a Spam with empties from Rotherhithe Road to Grove Park; stand there while making up the fire and bring the empties back to make up the 5 o'clock down, first stop Ashford. While we were waiting in the sidings at Grove Park, we heard the 4.20 Charing Cross – Hastings approaching. 'Blimey!' said Bill, 'who's that on the 4.20, pasteing the life out of that School?' Bill looked at his watch. 'He's nearly two minutes up.' The roar of a School being well and truly caned filled the station with its noise. We looked hard to see who in our No. 1 Gang was belting it along like this. Leaning out of the driver's side was the grinning face of Perce Chopping. Firing like a man in his early twenties was Tom Merrett, who was turned sixty, the white feather at the safety valves indicating that, in spite of Perce's heavy handling, Tom had got the needle on 220. . . .

When our turn came around for the 7.34 down, I told Bill that he would be having a new fireman for a week, while I got married. We walked up to London Bridge to relieve our men there and take the train down to Ashford. Upon arrival at London Bridge, Bill and I had a cup of tea, before going up to No. 3 Platform for our train. I finished my drink and Bill said he would be along in a minute. I walked on ahead, my ex-army gas-mask bag on my shoulder; in this I used to carry a tea-can, headcode and rule book, sandwiches and clean wipers. We had an Arthur going down, the usual motive power for this train, and called at Sevenoaks, Tonbridge, then all stations to Ashford. We had our break in The Kent Arms and I noticed that Bill was carrying a small parcel in his coat. Coming back we had the usual 'N' class and a short train, so I made up a good fire and prepared to sit down all the way to Paddock wood. 'Right,' said Bill. 'You drive, I'll fire.' He had a big grin on his face, knowing that there was no firing to do, so he sat down on my side and watched the road ahead. We got into Bricklayers Arms and were actually relieved on the coal stage. Bill fumbled inside his coat and produced the parcel. 'Here you are, Mick – a little something for you and your future missus! They're useful, good quality and initialled. I hope you will be pleased with them.' I was moved by Bill's thoughtfulness and thanked him. At home I unwrapped the parcel and found two cups and saucers, plus two tea plates; as Bill had said, they were initialled in green, S.R. . . .

As already mentioned, there had been some changes when I returned to Bricklayers Arms. Harry Packham had retired and in his place was Charles Boarer, who was appointed 'shed master', a term alien to Southern ears, but one officially replacing that of Superintendent. British Railways, after the locomotive exchanges of 1948, had begun to try and merge the four big railways together into one bigger family. Various liveries were tried out – 'plum-and-spilt-milk' for coaching stock was replaced with what was known as 'blood-and-custard'. One Schools had a large British Railways totem inscribed on the tender – but it looked terrible and no more were painted that way. Eventually, the lion and wheel emblem appeared (first, I believe, on the West Country class).

The old-style Locomotive Inspectors were giving way to a newer, more approachable type of man. George Russell, one of the drivers at Bricklayers Arms, became one and showed that the wearing of a black mackintosh and bowler hat did not necessarily mean he had joined the usual impersonal (even if dedicated) band. The old style of Inspector would ride on the driver's side, speak only a few words to him and none at all to the fireman. One Sunday, Bill and I were pass to Hastings to bring up an excursion. In the loco at St. Leonards, was 'L1', No. 31783, which was one of ours and had a bad reputation for steaming. I was not the only fireman to have S.O.S. written on the driver's ticket as an explanation for making an unscheduled stop when firing her. I tightened the smokebox door, raked out the ashpan, made up the fire and shovelled forward only the best coal, in fact did everything to try to ensure we had the best possible start. We backed onto our train – ten S.E.C.R. 'Bird Cage' coaches. A few minutes before starting time, onto the footplate climbed George Russell. 'I'm going to ride up with you and your mate, Bill,' he said. 'Coming down this morning, they had a bit of trouble getting steam with this lady.' I put my spoke in. 'This is the only one I have ever stopped with – in 1949 that was!' 'Stopping short of steam is all part of becoming a better engineman, in the long run,' responded George, with a smile. I was surprised – I expected a look of disapproval at least.

Anyway, off we went and up the hill to Battle. I had the fire well alight under the door and thought I had everything going fine, but as we neared Battle back went the pressure from 180 to 160 or so. George took over the shovel and looked into the fire. 'Don't put any more over the front for the next three rounds, Mick – let it thin out!' I did as I was told and round our 'L1' came and we had no shortage of steam to The Wells (Tunbridge Wells); after that, of course, it was downhill all the way to London.

Reverting to the Locomotive Exchanges of 1948, many Southern enginemen were disappointed that the Schools and Lord Nelsons were not considered suitable to be included. Everyone was convinced that a School would have easily managed the timing of 'The Bristolian' with its featherweight load on the billiard-table run out of Paddington. South Eastern men had had the Lord Nelsons before the war and with the expert firing these engines demanded – and got – they did magnificent work on the boat trains. I used to spend my holidays at Bournemouth and have timed several runs where 95 m.p.h. was reached, with only a quiet 'eight beats to the bar' at the exhaust. After the war, of course, the Nelsons migrated to the Western Section, being shedded at Nine Elms, Eastleigh and Bournemouth. Happily, No. 850 *Lord Nelson* is now included in the British Rail steam programme for passenger trains – fifty-five years after she was born!

Whilst I was away in the army, some of the old faces had gone. One was 'Blood' Wales, a large, portly driver who would get each new fireman paired with him to do all his oiling. On the 'H' class tanks he worked on in the Old Man's Gang it was difficult for him to get into the motions, if not impossible! Another character was 'Death' Harvey whose unfortunate nickname (which never seemed to bother him) arose from his exceptionally pale, wax-like complexion. In or about 1948, the government was concerned about the growing number of road deaths and large posters appeared everywhere, each depicting a sad-faced widow, wearing mourning clothes. In big letters these exhorted the public to KEEP DEATH OFF THE ROAD (a driver or fireman who was said to be off the road, of course, was one confined to yard duty only). Thereafter, Driver Harvey used to point proudly to these posters and say, 'That means me!'

Some time after Nationalisation, a 'League Table' was shown in every depot on the Southern, setting out the top and bottom depots, based on timekeeping per thousand train miles. A few minutes lost on several short runs to Hastings, for example, could play havoc with a depot's 'league' position. The idea was to give an incentive to bring one's own depot up to the top. By the time our new shed master, Charles Boarer, arrived at Bricklayers Arms in May 1950, the depot was well down the league, and morale was not at its best. Heavily laden 'business expresses' out of Cannon Street were constantly being checked, in order to let the electrics go by from Charing Cross. Restarting heavy trains on the sharp left-hand, check-railed curve here lost these tightly-timed steam trains a lot of time and then they lost their pathway, to the frustration of the engine crew. Charles Boarer decided to do something about it and took the unusual step of riding on the footplate for some days to see where the fault for these delays lay. By 1951, our depot was on the up-and-up, thanks to the renewed efforts by all staff and in no small measure due to the interest taken by our new guv'nor. The Southern, of course, had been an electric train-minded system since the late 1920s and it was held that an electric could always 'get out of the way' quicker than one that was steam-hauled. What tended to be overlooked was that the steam locomotive had not the acceleration powers of an electric train and quickly lost its pathway.

The second cause was suitable engine availability. With a stud of 110 Spams, 40 Schools, 16 Nelsons, 74 Arthurs and 30 Merchant Navies, plus four B.R. Standard Britannias, there should have been enough main line engines on the Eastern and Western sections of the Southern. However, the availability of the Bulleid Pacifics was always a big question, since their problems were many. More than a few books and articles have been written on the subject of Bulleid's Pacifics. On a good day, they had no equal. Fresh out of the shops, the chain-driven valve gear in its oil bath provided a crisp response to the regulator. Once the chain and its associated fittings 'gave', however, the timing was out and the reverser readings a joke. What puzzled many enginemen was the fact that so many were built, even when these bad faults had been evident in the first few produced. The absence of dampers also wasted endless fuel and to have a Spam in fit condition to tackle the climb to Bridge 179 or the 1 in 64 climb out of Victoria was a job in itself – trying to avoid smoke and blowing-off. Various dodges were resorted to, such as opening the steam heater pipes and venting off say 50 lbs pressure of steam to keep the loco quiet or leaving the front of the grate bare of fire, (which in turn led to the inevitable leaks in the firebox). The constant leakage of thick oil onto the track caused what became jocularly known as ' Spam Start', though it is true experienced handling of the regulator by 'pumping it' helped to reduce slipping. The rocking-grate, when used on the road, frequently got stuck in the open position, causing more problems, whilst the look-out from the footplate could only be described as fair, even after improvements. The weakness of the blow-down fittings and the inherent dangers have also already been described. It is interesting to note that a shed which had six Schools, Nelsons or Arthurs was allocated one fitter, yet for only three Spams, one fitter was deemed necessary! Dan Knight, one of the Western section's popular inspectors, said of them that they were designed by a brilliant engineer – but what a pity he was not a *practical* engineer.

Bulleid, who retired in October 1947, also designed the 'double-decker' electric train, fitting 508 seats in a four-car set as opposed to the 420 in the 1946 4-SUB sets. But had he been 'a practical railway engineer', he would have realised that, with only the same number of doors as the conventional train, it would take much longer to detrain and entrain passengers in the 20 seconds that e.m.u.s. were allowed for their station stops on schedules timed in half-minutes! Thankfully for Southern commuters, only two of these 4-car 'DD' sets were built.

As for his 'Leader' class, Bulleid certainly never considered the working temperature for the fireman enclosed in the centre of the engine. I recall seeing a Brighton fireman emerge from his 'hell-hole' dripping with sweat on a winter's day and looking 'all-in', even though he had only worked from Eridge!

One driver is said to have asked the exhausted stoker what he would have liked to have had in his firing compartment – the fireman finished his third cup of water and said one word 'Bulleid'. . . .

No one could say, however, that Bulleid was not a genius in many ways. His coaching stock for the Bournemouth services were an excellent design – roomy, comfortable and good riding. His 4-SUB 4111 series were no less excellent and he brought open compartments back into popularity.

The unreliability of the Spams caused endless problems that could have been avoided if more Nelsons had been built instead. It was all very well building engines that had no technical equal, but railways run on consistent reliability, not 'flash-in-the-pan' occasions. As is well known, the breaking of a driving axle on a Merchant Navy, while descending Crewkerne bank at speed early in 1953, caused the temporary withdrawal of all the Bulleid Pacifics, leaving Southern motive power in a depleted state. Eastern Region B1 4–6–0s were drafted in to fill the gaps and Ramsgate and 'the Lane' crews coped admirably with their strange new mounts until the Pacifics were checked for flaws.

In contrast, the reliability of the Schools had only once been questioned and that was back in 1934, when 910 *Merchant Taylors* dropped her inside connecting rod, due to metal fatigue. From then on, all of the class had coupling and connecting rods made of 'Vibrac' nickel-steel, something which gave them a most distinctive sound when running without steam-on. From then on, there were no serious problems and the Schools' reliability was such that they displaced the 4–6–0 King Arthurs on the 108-mile non-stop run of 'The Bournemouth Limited' until the outbreak of World War II caused the end of that service. From 1931 until the end of steam, on the tortuous, heavily graded and twisting route to Hastings, the Schools were in charge. This was the route which had prompted their design, a modified 'Lord Nelson' which surprised even its designer, Richard Maunsell, with its success. The King Arthurs, especially the small tender versions (793–806), did splendid work on the Eastern section and like the big-tender ones, could be started on full regulator, when the need arose, without losing their feet.

Looking back then, what were the causes of delays that so infuriated the fare-paying public and the London evening papers? Poor coal was partly to blame and certainly some firemen seemed unable to cope with the demands made on them. I have before me an article written by Cecil J. Allen to which a fireman, whom 'CJ' quoted, wrote, 'With the new tanks if the pressure drops below 150 lbs, the brakes leak on'. No wonder his driver lost time! However, the majority of regular firemen in the No. 1 and No. 2 links were competent or their elderly drivers would not have tolerated them, and the main cause for the late running of steam trains was the fitting in between the world's most intensive electric train service of the slower steam train. A door not properly shut on the 20-second station stop perhaps caused another 20-second delay to an electric. One passenger being choosy as to which coach he selected to ride home in could cause another period of delay – result, the train almost three-quarters of a minute late passing Borough Market Junction, so a heavy steam train was checked or, very often, brought to a stand and lost not three-quarters of a minute, but nearer three by the time the road was set, signals cleared and the train restarted on that sharp, check-railed curve. Other electrics following started to 'bunch up' and in order to clear them, the next steam train was held up. Of course we have only covered down trains. Up trains crossing into Cannon Street and in front of down trains from Charing Cross lost their delicately-timed paths and so that chaos grew. The same problems are with us today incidentally, though the grouping of Cannon Street and Charing Cross trains outside New Cross has helped to minimise delays.

The Season Ticket Holders' Association regularly deluged Waterloo with their dissatisfaction at the apparently cavalier way that their members' services were handled. Eventually one of them was given the opportunity of travelling down on the footplate to get the driver's view, which brought home the hold-ups at Borough Market Junction and the efforts of the engine crew to regain time (more about this run in the next chapter). It is ironic that the successful electrification of the Southern Railway, which helped the development of rural areas into residential suburbia, resulting into morning and evening peaks with little traffic in between, has caused such financial and operating problems.

Reverting to the partnership I enjoyed with Driver W. T. Snell, it was amid such a background of problems that enginemen endeavoured to not only keep time but to regain it, when lost through circumstances no fault of their own.

In the middle of December, Bill and I had an Army special up from Folkestone to London Bridge, via 'the Old Road'. It was quite a pleasant afternoon when we left Folkstone and with nine coaches and a School, an easy run. At Tonbridge we joined the old South Eastern main line to Redhill and passed through Godstone. Approaching Merstham, the sky was grey and when we emerged from the tunnel, it was getting dark, although it was barely 3.45 p.m. 'Looks as if we are running into a bit of fog, mate,' said Bill.

By the time we reached Purley, the fog was certainly thick, with a yellow look about it, and we had reduced speed to a crawl. By South Croydon, we were down to no more than walking pace. Landmarks so often passed and so familiar were swallowed in a dense, sound-deadening fog, the kind Londoners hated. This was a real 'pea souper' which was what later to become known as 'The Great Smog' of London. East Croydon station was just a murky shadow. We stopped in the station for me to climb the post carrying the colour light signals to see what aspect was showing – two yellows. We moved on slowly, straining to see the next signal, the ringing of the School's coupling and connecting rods being all the sound we could hear. Trains passing us seemed muffled for the fog muffled all sounds. We crept slowly up to a red light ahead, almost over our chimney. Bill dropped the handle and we stopped. The light of the signal seemed to change to a dirty brown and for a moment I thought it was yellow, but no, it was still red, the fog almost obscuring the powerful beam.

It took us 45 minutes from East Croydon to reach London Bridge where, thank goodness, our relief was waiting. All we had to do now was get home! If I had known what lay ahead, I would have walked. . . . Bill went over to No. 2 Platform to get a train to Mottingham, I went to the Central side to get a Crystal Palace or Epsom Downs train. The platforms were full beyond belief as crowds of would-be passengers continued to enter the station. Few trains were now leaving – and even fewer coming in!

I eventually got to the front end of the 5.23 to Crystal Palace and, since it was so full, it was impossible to get into the train. I asked the motorman if I could ride with him, a request he readily agreed to. We followed the 5.20 Epsom Downs out, which was booked fast to Norwood Junction. We left London Bridge on 'two yellows' and the motorman put the train into series and the pair of us pressed our faces against the cab lights, to see as far ahead as possible. The motorman commented that he had been on the Central Section for many years but had never seen fog like this. He shut off power and let her run. The landmarks and associated trackside noises, normally so familiar, seemed to have vanished; after a while he muttered, 'I'm lost, mate! Lost in my own backyard!'

He applied the brakes and we slowed down to a crawl. In the silent gloom around us, the only sound was the wheels going over the track joints. The motorman gave her another 5 lbs of air and we came down to maybe two or three miles an hour. Above us loomed a yellow light – what signal was that, we wondered? We continued to move slowly along. If that was the third signal out of London Bridge, we should have crossed several sets of points by now. The signals were approximately four hundred yards apart – the rail joints 20 yards apart – count 20 joints and we should be close to the next. We counted up to 18, he applied the brakes, then released them. Two more joints, and he stopped. We opened the cab doors either side and peered out – nothing to be seen but thick fog. It was unnerving, more so for the driver even than for me. He worked over this section maybe a dozen times a day, yet had no idea where we now were!

He opened the controller into 'shunt' and got the train moving, but very slowly. The train was packed and we could hear the crowd of people in the guard's compartment behind us, commenting on the lack of progress. In itself this was a strange occurrence, since the public rarely held audible conversations, being usually immersed in the newspapers.

We rolled slowly along with the silence broken only by the wheels and the Westinghouse air compressor, occasionally bursting into its monotonous pumping. Suddenly, immediately in front of us loomed up a rectangular white plate – the blank headcode plate of the last coach of the 5.20 to Epsom Downs! The motorman beside me let go the 'dead man's' and gave full emergency stop on the brake valve but it was too late. There was an almighty Bang! as we struck the train in front and all lights in our train went out. The door behind us, leading to the guard's brake, flew open and passengers were thrown forward into our cab. Screams from women were mixed with shouts from male passengers and general commotion. I heard myself saying, 'Calm down! Just a bump, nothing to get excited about. Please get back into the guard's compartment and keep quiet.'

Both the motorman and I had banged our face on the cab lights but apart from bruised foreheads and my aching nose, we were alright. Our guard threw the breaker switch and the lights came on again, at which the motorman said that some of our shoes must still be on the third rail or the train lights would be so bright. He got out and went forward to confer with the motorman of the 5.20, whom he found examining his train to see if there was any derailment. Two or three passengers came into the driving cab and asked if there was anything they could do to assist, and I told them that calming one or two hysterical female travellers would be the most helpful thing they could do. The motorman returned, showing signs of delayed shock for a minute or two, but then he was back to normal. He asked if I would walk back along the train and ensure we were 'all wheels on the road'. Many passengers had cuts and bleeding noses and bruises. When I neared the end of the train, I realised just how many had been bruised or injured by the seats breaking away – the bolts holding them to the floors had snapped – throwing them forward. I reached the last coach and climbed up into the crowded guard's compartment. Although the line was fully protected by track circuiting, the guard had, quite rightly, left the train in order to put down detonators in case another motorman should miss the signals to our rear. Dressed in bowler hat and clutching an umbrella, but with his suit a bit dirty, a city type was proudly holding the brake valve handle of the emergency brake. He told me that the guard had left him in charge while he placed detonators on the line behind us. 'If you attempt to move the train before he returns, I have his authority to pull this handle,' he said. 'Good man, keep hold of the handle and tell the guard that when I return to the cab, we will make two brake applications. If the guard has not returned, make one long brake application like this.' I pulled his hand down on the handle and applied the brake. I put it back into the 'off' position. 'Have you got it, sir?' He nodded rather solemnly and repeated my instructions, adding, 'And what if the guard has returned?' I answered, 'Repeat my signal – two applications.' 'Got it,' he replied. 'You can rely on me, driver!'

With that, I set off back along the other side of the train, to ensure that all the collecting shoes were in contact with the live rail. It was at this point that I discovered we were on a bridge and I knew then where we were – close to Bricklayers Arms Junction.

Ambulances were waiting for us at New Cross Gate and with some reasonable organisation all the casualties were got away in good time but it was seven o'clock before I got out of the crawling train at Forest Hill and groped my way home in the 'smog'.

Electric train seats were later welded to the floor rather than bolted and eventually the Clean Air Bill was passed, with London becoming a smokeless zone. Smog no longer troubles it – or railwaymen!

Bill and I continued to work through the 12 week roster. I noted that each time Bill undid his packet of sandwiches he would murmur to himself, 'Wonder what I've got to eat today?' He would open up one corner of a sandwich, solemnly commenting, 'Gawd Blimey! Mouse's food again!' as he surveyed a cheese sandwich. Eventually I was driven to ask him who was making him cheese sandwiches every day. He answered, 'I do – it's all I can find in the 'fridge!'

We came home pass in a boat train from Dover one day. In one of the old panelled second class coaches, over the window in the door, was written the warning: 'Ne se pencher au dehors'. I was unable to translate this, so I asked Bill. He stroked his chin and looked at me in mock disgust. 'I thought they had taught you French at school – it's easy.' He pointed to the words and slowly spelled it out – 'Don't pinch your fingers in the doors!' Bill went on to tell me he had learned some

French when he joined the Army in 1914. Bill did most of his service in Egypt and many was the tale he had to tell of that distant land. He also recalled how some London bus horses were drafted to pull guns to the front line in Flanders. They refused to budge when harnessed, in spite of every effort by the gun-crews. Then someone produced a bell and rang it twice and off went the horses, no doubt trained only to stop and start to a conductor's bell!

CHAPTER SEVEN

Top Link

A NEW SET of rosters was posted at this time and I was moved into No. 1 link. This was the top one at Bricklayers Arms and was sometimes referred to as 'the Honour and Glory Link', since most of its duties consisted of a bare eight-hour day, with little overtime or mileage payments. Most of the 'turns' were of the 'step onto the footplate, work, and step off again' variety, with little preparation or disposal to do, but the lower down the links the more opportunity for overtime existed. From the driver's point of view, by the time they reached No. 1 link, they were likely to be close to sixty years of age and had no wish to do overtime, since the business of running top link trains was a tiring and responsible enough job in itself. At one time, No. 1 link had several mileage turns, which helped to boost pay packets. A day's work, on the running line, was set at 140 miles and for every ten miles in excess of this figure, an extra hour's pay was made, so that a return trip to Dover (78 miles each way), earned the crew an extra hour and a half pay. A 'Rounder' from Charing Cross to Ramsgate via Dover and back to Victoria totalled 180 miles, which at the end of the week made a handsome wage. In addition to this, these mileage turns were often completed in under six hours actual duty time, resulting in a short working day. Drivers' (and firemen's) pay reached a top rate after five years and considering it took drivers some forty or so years to reach the top link, the mileage payments were considered as a 'proficiency' payment. Over the years, economies had been made which resulted in the whittling away of the mileage turns, which gave rise to the sarcastic reference to the top link that they worked for honour and glory alone.

A top link fireman would eventually pass as a 'Passed Fireman', come out of that link and go to the bottom as 'Spare Driver', until he became an appointed driver, then start the long climb up through the links until he too, nearing sixty years of age, would reach the pinnacle of his career. There were no short cuts to main line work in the days of steam.

The top link, when I joined it, had some superb drivers among its ranks. Ted Jakes, one of the former ex-New Cross men, was dubbed 'an Arthur Master', in view of his skill in getting the best out of what I for one considered to be a much maligned class of engine. Most South Eastern men had a poor opinion of the Arthurs and often referred to them as 'one-legged', from the heavy beat followed by a lighter beat from the exhaust. Ted, brought up on Atlantics, 13s and B4Xs, took to the Arthurs and made the working of them an art. His handling of the Schools was also classic.

Perce Collins, whom we have already met in these pages, loved the Schools, as most Southern men did. These 4–4–0s of course, became a legend in their own time and it was a rarity if one failed to complete its allotted day's work. Perce, I remember, was amused by the idiosyncrasies and vagaries of the West Country/Battle of Britain 'Spams' and often remarked to me that you were never bored when you had a Spam, as you just didn't know what they would get up to next!

Another in the No. 1 link was old Alf King, a fragile-looking little man, but when he took the regulator of any engine – be it a School, an Arthur or a Pacific – he kept time, and if time was lost from any cause, he would regain it. The speciality of Death Harvey, whom we have also met before, was the Schools; he would restart one with the reversing gear in mid-gear position and slowly wind it forward until, as he put it, 'She found her stride.' Harvey had O.S. Nock ride with him on the Hastings run on a Schools, which the latter recorded in glowing terms, appreciating the skill with which the engine was handled.

My driver in No. 1 link was Harry Gillingham, who had a son at Bricklayers Arms also on the footplate. Our first turn together was with the 8.25 a.m. Charing Cross to Hastings. We relieved a pair from No. 4 link at London Bridge on 30933 *King's Canterbury* and had an easy run down to Tonbridge, where we were relieved. At Tonbridge loco we took out No. 30909 (a St. Leonards Schools) to the up sidings.

For a run on King Arthur No. 795 'Sir Dinadan', up with the Dover Mail – and a broken finger into the bargain, see page 53.

No. 10800 – the wonder diesel . . .

E3 No. 2459 and H class No. 1542 in the old shed at Bricklayers Arms.

There we stood the rest of the morning, as stand-by engine. We had to keep a big fire on, ready to take over any up train that might happen to have engine trouble. We watched the approach of each train with interest, of course. Harry would take a look at each approaching engine and say, 'No! He's alright, Mick, plenty of steam. Wait for the next one!' Eventually, however, we were called on to work up to Charing Cross with the 1.57 p.m. from Tonbridge (11.30 a.m. ex Ramsgate, via Dover), the train engine coming off the train and going into Tonbridge loco. Upon arrival at Charing Cross, we were relieved and that was our day's work – very mundane.

The following week was to prove a little more strenuous, however. We signed on at 4.5 p.m. and were pass to Cannon Street to relieve Bricklayers Arms men on a Schools, 30931 *King's Wimbledon*, to take the 5.6 p.m. to Hastings. Harry asked me if I knew much about the 5.6 and I replied that it was fast to Tunbridge Wells, as were the 6.3 and the 8.25 p.m. down to Hastings. He laughed. 'That's all you know about the 5.6, is it?' I thought a minute and then added, 'Oh! The London evening papers have had a few words about it losing time!' Harry smiled. 'Yes,' he said. 'Them *and* the season ticket holders!'

As mentioned earlier, in the early 1950s fewer people owned cars and many commuters relied upon buses for the last stage of their journey home. Harry recalled it being said that with coal at £5 per ton, it only took five first class 'Monthly Return' passengers to pay for the coal for our London to Hastings journey!

The previous week, on this duty, Charles Boarer, our shedmaster, had ridden down on the footplate, to satisfy himself that everything that could be done by the enginemen to arrive at 'The Wells' on time, had been attempted. Harry, however, said he had the remedy in his jacket pocket, and this would stop our late arrivals. At this point, we got the 'right away' but were thereafter stopped dead at Borough Market Junction – with the signal clearing the moment we had actually come to halt. Harry got our Schools moving again and took something from his pocket; he extended his left arm out of the cab, pointing at the signal box and from his hand dangled a small length of thick white cord, fashioned into a hangman's noose! 'My bloody remedy would be to hang the signalman here!' he shouted across towards the box, giving a long blast on the whistle at the same time to emphasise his comment. We went like the proverbial wind, but for no apparent reason were checked again by signals at New Cross. This spoiled our run up the beginning of the climb to Knockholt and lost us another minute. Furious at this, Harry shouted over to me that here was another signalman that wanted seeing to! Out came the noose again, with a blast on the whistle as we passed Parks Bridge box. We arrived at Tunbridge Wells four minutes late – getting a lost time ticket to prove it!

The next evening, we sat at Cannon Street sipping our tea, Harry reading an evening paper. 'Can't see our names in here,' he said ruefully, as he read out another letter of complaint to me. We got onto the same engine as the previous night, 30931 *King's Wimbledon*. She was a good 'un, no doubt there, and after a look at the fire, I took off my serge jacket, put it in the 'clothes cupboard', and stood the teacan on the glare-plate (usually known as the mantle-shelf). Then I joined Harry, leaning over the side of the cab, watching the passengers boarding the train. Walking up the platform was Inspector George Dunnett, one-time foreman at the Brick, and with him was a bowler-hatted individual attired in pin-striped suit and carrying a rolled umbrella. Inspector Dunnett introduced him as a member of the Season Ticket Holders' Association, who was going to ride down on the footplate with us. We shook hands and George Dunnett suggested that the man stand behind Harry – to keep well out of my shovel-swinging way, no doubt. The needle of the pressure gauge was just touching 220 as we got the 'right away' and with a beautifully clean start, 30931 pulled out of Cannon Street. Our visitor listened as George pointed to the signals on the curve which, true to form, were red, even though our start out of Cannon Street had been a little slower than the previous evening, hoping that the signals would clear before we came to a stand. The signal then changed to green and we pulled slowly away, Harry cursing under his breath but refraining from exhibiting his white noose on this occasion. With the cut-off on 40 per cent, we roared through No. 3 Platform at London Bridge, the Inspector shouting to our visitor we were already over two minutes down. The visitor scribbled unsteadily in a little notebook he had and nodded his head.

I fired steadily, making sure that the fire under the door was kept bright, for these big-chimney Schools did not like the fire 'blacked out' under the door the same way those with the small chimneys did. Over The Arches, picking up speed rapidly, *King's Wimbledon* was steaming beautifully.

Another seven into the firebox, then blower on for the approaching low bridge at New Cross station and the short Tanners Hill Tunnel. Cut off on 30 per cent now, regulator fully open in the first port and a blast on the whistle. Inspector Dunnett caught hold of the visitor's arm to stop him leaning out as we tore through New Cross, at 5.15 p.m., still almost three minutes down. St. Johns starter was a green – an open palm to Harry, who nodded in acknowledgement and put 30931 into the second valve. George told our visitor to hold on as we took the righthander under the Nunhead flyover and attacked Hither Green bank. We passed a heavily-loaded electric, George getting a wave from the motorman, whom he knew. We passed Hither Green loco and then Chislehurst, two minutes down. I offered our guest a drink of tea from the tea can but he shook his head, being too fastidious, I suppose, to join in with us. He was holding onto the grab-rail behind Harry's head, with a 'green liner' protecting his hand (a white spongecloth with a green thread running through it) and was evidently beginning to enjoy his trip.

George pointed out the site of the old sidings at Orpington, known as Hill 60 sidings where, during the First World War, ambulance trains unloaded hundreds of wounded troops, survivors of that terrible battle, for transfer into Orpington Hospital. Harry called out to me. 'Keep a look out for an Inspector here!' as we tore through Orpington station, but George chipped in that he must be busy today – normally, of course, George would have been standing on duty on the platform here to observe the progress of passing trains.

Through Polhill Tunnel, downhill through Sevenoaks and into the almost two mile length of Sevenoaks Tunnel we went, whistle screaming for the first quarter of a mile, then again in the middle of the tunnel and again for a quarter of a mile before we emerged at a good 85 m.p.h. Blower on, doors open as the regulator was shut for the fast-approaching Tonbridge curve and the coal on the tender was given a good watering to keep down the dust, being blown off the tender into the engine cab by the slip-stream rebounding from the front of the first coach.

We passed Tonbridge at 5.44½, still one minute late, and then attacked the sharp right hand curve up towards Tunbridge Wells. This had a ruling gradient of 1 in 100, commencing with an initial climb from Tonbridge Yard at 1 in 47 easing to 1 in 53, then 1 in 95 to 1 in 97 by High Brooms station. We arrived at 'The Wells' at 5.55, still a minute down, but our guest was obviously pleased by the run. His verdict was that 'Waterloo' should see that steam trains were not halted at Borough Market Junction, as he agreed with us that the main cause for continued late running was not due to any laxity on the part of engine crews. For the rest of the week, and henceforward, the 5.6 got a clear road round

Borough Market Junction and Harry's noose remained in his pocket. We never knew if it was this, or the result of our footplate visitor's report, that was responsible . . . .

A new innovation for Bricklayers Arms at this time was the provision of a hut with a man in it to record the names of drivers taking engines out of the depot or into it, night and day. This man became generally known to us as 'him' and since the depot had managed without a 'him' for something like a hundred years, his job seemed pointless. His duty was to inform the signalmen at No. 3 box the destination of out-going engines – although the men there had managed, up to his arrival, to send engines down the branch line without losing one! We regarded the newcomer as a spy, checking on the drivers' booked time of arrival, as recorded on their daily 'Drivers' Bills'. Now, quite a few years ago, there had been a well-known driver at the Brick with the unusual name of Sponnheimer, and since the provision of the hut and its occupant, when leaving or entering, quite a few drivers gave 'Sponnheimer' as their name. It was also recorded that we had drivers with the names 'Montgomery', 'Rommel', etc – and even some Polish swear words. This grew so bad that an official notice was posted requesting drivers to give their correct names. As it happened, the distrust by enginemen of this innovation stemmed from several concurrent attempts by Time and Motion Study men (colloquially known as the Razor Gang) to try to eliminate overtime. However, since most engines had barely an hour to be put away, got ready and out of the depot from the time of arrival on the coal stage, the Razor Gang gave up and left. The Preparation and Disposal crews were in fact doing two hours work in one and no one could ask more than that. Eventually the 'hims' working round the clock were replaced with drivers who had retired and since these knew the name of most drivers at the depot, the game was over.

On Derby Day, the Queen and Prince Philip traditionally travelled to Tattenham Corner by train, with Stewarts Lane shed providing the engine and crew. One of the Schools, 30915 *Brighton*, was the motive power for this in my day and she received what was commonly known as 'the treatment' for the Royal occasion. The cab roof was painted white, as were the wheel rims, whilst all pipes were scoured. The buffers were burnished and the vacuum and steam heating hoses painted silver. Her paintwork, needless to say, was spotless, and she looked a picture. As was the case for all Royal specials, stand-by engines were

41298 was one of the so-called 'Teddy Bears' – fine locomotives.

A pair of 'bacon slicers' (Nos. 80045 and 80046) outside Brighton Works.

'Midland' 4MT 2–6–4T No. 42091 in Stewarts Lane yard.

placed at strategic points. Harry and I were given 30933 *King's Canterbury* to take to East Croydon and await the passing of the Royal Train. Our cleaners also set to work on 30933, bringing her up to a condition not far short of 30915 and even our hose pipes were painted silver, though the cab roof remained its normal black. We ran light to East Croydon and stood to attention as the Royal Train went by. Afterwards, not being required, we ran light to Stewarts Lane.

At this period, Bricklayers Arms lost the 11 p.m. Brighton – London Bridge mail train as well as the 3.23 London Bridge – Brighton paper train, both ex-New Cross workings. Under the new arrangements, Brighton men came up with the 11 p.m. and worked the 3.23 down, usually with a West Country which was diagrammed for the two duties in place of a Schools as formerly. However, we still had the 5 p.m. down, which had been a Bricklayers Arms working for over thirty years. This was the train involved in the disaster at Riverhead, with 2–6–4T No. 800 *River Cray* which led to the complete re-ballasting of the Southern Railway with Meldon Quarry ballast in place of the smokebox ash and Dungeness pebbles then usual on the South Eastern section.

The 'Five o'clock' was a Spam turn, fast to Ashford from Cannon Street in 64 minutes. Our first run on this train was with 34088, and passing New Cross, Harry called me to his side of the footplate and pointed to the reversing lever – it was 10 per cent in reverse gear! Nevertheless we passed Orpington one minute early, the boiler pressure remaining between 260–275 all the way. However, as usual with a Spam, it was a case of 'keep shovelling' even when running downhill through Polhill and Sevenoaks tunnels, as the draught caused by the lack of dampers ate the fire away just as if the regulator was open.

We had heard that a week or two previously, one fireman on the 'Five o'clock' had decided to give his fire a 'lift-up' to get it burning to perfection and, being reluctant to use the 'rocking grate' for reasons already outlined, he used the small rake and then threw it back into the recess, alongside the tender top. This was near New Cross. Upon arrival at Ashford, a locomotive inspector came up and asked the fireman if he had a full set of fire-irons. Doubtless a bit puzzled, the fireman checked and found that he had a dart and scoop, but his rake seemed to have gone missing. . . . The inspector then told him that the rake in question had fallen from the engine and welded itself to the live-rail outside New Cross station, bringing all traffic to a standstill as a result! I believe he and his driver had an uncomfortable session on the carpet at

Waterloo, a few days after this incident!

The live rail was one that demanded respect at all times. I remember seeing a thoughtless fireman empty a bucket of water from the footplate down onto the live rail – the bucket went one way, the fireman was thrown across the footplate the other! Some years before this incident, I was working on a ballast train at Camberwell Junction. The platelayers were taking out the old ballast and replacing it with new, which was evenly distributed between the sleepers with large metal forks. The current, which had been off all night, was switched on to permit the passage of the first electric train and the fireman ganger in charge blew a whistle as a warning and shouted, 'Careful, lads, the juice is on now!' One platelayer seemed to be getting the tines of his fork perilously close to the live rail as we watched and a moment or two later there was a flash of blue, a cloud of dust and the man stumbled away. He was lucky to be alive, but as it was he recovered after sitting down for a few minutes.

Another time I crossed the live rail at New Cross Gate one day during a thunderstorm and the heavy rain, running down the back of my railway mackintosh in a long stream connected with the live rail. I saw a blue flash, felt a jolt and had a nasty headache for an hour or so.

One evening, with the five o'clock down, we were held up for a while between St. Johns and Hither Green, spoiling our run at the bank. Harry, who still carried his effective noose at all times, exhibited it to the signalmen concerned. In something of a rage he decided to make up time but our engine, 34086 *219 Squadron* thought otherwise, and started to prime. This was always a potentially dangerous situation, since water from the boiler was ejected through the chimney and if it found its way into the cylinders could cause a bent rod. Harry shut the regulator and opened the cylinder cocks whilst I opened the firehole doors, since the last thing we wanted now was blowing-off. The water in the gauge glasses was a mass of bubbles, making it impossible to tell the level in the boiler, so I kept the injector on. When Harry opened the regulator again with the cylinder cocks still open, 34086 cleared herself and we ran with half-a-glass of water for the rest of the journey, after some very uncomfortable moments. 'Wants a good shed day!' Harry shouted over, meaning that the boiler needed washing out, to remove the scale and sediment which caused the priming.

The following evening, we had the same engine and, as we passed Hither Green station, the priming started again. Our flow of bad language, even in these permissive days, could not be set down on paper! The net result was we lost three minutes to Ashford and received the inevitable 'Guard's Lost Time Ticket'. On this Driver Gillingham wrote, 'Priming. Worse than the night before!'

Harry put in a report about 34086 when we reached the shed. The next night, there was 34086 again and obviously not washed out. Harry was angry and when we returned that evening, went in to see the foreman. He came out with one of his classic remarks to that personage, saying, 'I do not normally swear or make remarks in bad taste, but I must say I feel that your parents were casual acquaintances on a night-sleeper!'

The London East Divisional Superintendent's Office was situated at Orpington, which issued – amongst a lot of other paper – the duplicated Special Notices I once carried back to Bricklayers Arms as a cleaner/messenger. To all enginemen, however, L.E.D.S.O. was known simply as CON-trol, (with the accent on the first syllable). There were, in fact, three controls, one for each section – the others being at Woking for the Western Division, and at Redhill for the Central Division.

The old Orpington Control was a collection of wooden huts and an old restaurant car, pressed into service as an office. Anyone who was on the Southern of importance, at one time or another was at Orpington Control and for this reason some main line steam trains called there. It was an unwritten rule that any train from London that was in trouble for steam should stop at Orpington to avoid holding up following trains, for here the four tracks merged into two, one down and one up. Of course, any train stopping on the doorstep of Control might well have descend upon it an Inspector or other high-up of the Locomotive Running Department. Unscheduled stops at Orpington were, therefore, a rarity.

One of the few main line trains that were booked to stop at Orpington was the 4.20 Charing Cross to Hastings. Upon our arrival one day, an official boarded our engine, showing the requisite footplate permit. I could not stop the Schools from blowing off and the official, ignoring me, remarked to Harry, 'Your engine is blowing off, driver.' My mate replied promptly, 'I'm not surprised – making us stop three miles from the top of the climb from St. Johns! I'm glad you agree with me!' Before the official could think of a reply to this we were off and with the cut-off on 50 per cent, we stormed away from the station with me firing for all I was worth. As usual, I paused from my labours to wave to the nurses down in Orpington Hospital, a custom for all crews. Our official guest asked Harry who I was waving to, and received the masterly reply, 'His sister is one of the nurses.' This evidently satisfied our passenger, but I must say it came as a surprise to me that I had a sister, let alone one who was a nurse!

Much criticism occurred at this time about the dirty state of locomotives used on these morning and evening business trains. After the end of the Second World War, not enough youngsters joined the railway service in the London area to keep the cleaning programme fulfilled. Remember too that on the Hastings run, a distance of just over 62 miles, over seven miles was in tunnels – or 12 per cent of the journey! The 77 mile run to Dover Priory also took a loco through just 66 yards short of seven miles of tunnels.

Many of these numerous tunnels on the Southern were notoriously wet and a combination of smoke, cinders, ash and moisture soon rendered locomotives grimy. Coming in or out of Victoria, for example, Penge Tunnel had a 'dirty' reputation, soon dulling the polish given by engine cleaners at Stewarts Lane or at Dover and, of course, Ramsgate depot too.

As a finale, let me describe one typical run with my mate Harry. This was on the 7.23 London Bridge to Margate via Tonbridge, Deal and Sandwich, first stop Orpington. Originally, this train started from Holborn Viaduct and for this reason had, as motive power, the heaviest engine allowed to cross Blackfriars Bridge, one of the rebuilt 'E1' Coppertops. When the start out of Holborn was changed in favour of London Bridge, the motive power remained the same. These 4–4–0s had a long, narrow firebox, the depth of which was shallow. Many a fireman had trouble with these, through not keeping a very watchful eye on the fire. This tended to shake forward and build up under the brick arch, thereby stopping coal being shot to the front end of the box.

On one particular occasion Harry took off his serge jacket, placed it carefully in the clothes cupboard and came over to my side. Picking up the shovel he waved me over to the driver's side with the cheery comment. 'I'll provide the steam, you get us to Orpington on time!'

The 'E1' had steam-reverse of the dead-beat variety, which was slow to move, enabling the driver to select the best cut-off, almost as if using a hand-wound reverse. At the off, I opened the regulator fully into the first port, then snapped it shut as the wheels took hold, opened her up again and we were away, with a clean start. Harry, I noticed was watching me and as I saw him smile I gathered he was pleased. Then he opened the fire-hole doors and got down to firing. The 'E1' had a sharp bark, not as loud as an 'L' Class 'German' or an 'L1', but a good sharp bark nevertheless. It was this that used to mislead some inexperienced firemen into thinking their engine was being much more heavily worked than was actually the case. I sat on the little tip-up seat and with the cut-off on 30 per cent we hurried across 'The Arches'. Harry was firing well, and put the injector on at Peak Freans, when the water had come down an inch; with the regulator open this meant that the boiler was half full. New Cross, Harry had time to pull the whistle chain and I turned the blower on for the overbridge and Tanners Hill Tunnel risk of a blow-back, then turned it almost off. Harry, on the fireman's side, called out 'green' for the two intermediate signals between New Cross and St. Johns, situated on the left-hand side of the engine. I saw that St. Johns starter was a green on my side and under the flyover we went into the climb. I increased the cut-off to 35 per cent, feeling the increase in power as I did so. Harry continued to fire almost lazily, with the needle remaining steady on 180. He watered the coal, singing quietly to himself, and then resumed firing. Our 'E1' was fairly barking along and we passed Grove Park at about 40 m.p.h. Approaching Orpington, Harry put the second injector on, to avoid blowing-off in the station. I ran in carefully and we stopped at 7.47, just on time. He shut off one injector as our engine had dropped back to 170, then looked up and down the platform, which was on his side of the footplate. 'No bowler hats about,' he confirmed. A minute later came the green flag and we set off for our next call at Sevenoaks.

Next, I had to stop right for water at Tonbridge, although with the water crane on my side that was not too difficult. I scrambled up onto the tender to put the pipe in and let Harry turn the water on; meanwhile I threw some coal forward ready for our 34-minute dash to Ashford. I had rather expected he would take over the regulator now, as he had fired over the hardest part of the trip. Water crane turned off and tender full, I climbed back onto the footplate. 'I enjoyed that,' I said, referring to the trip, but Harry raised his eyebrow and replied, 'You haven't got to Ashford yet, mate! Let's see what you can do on the race-track bit!'

Most trains running non-stop between Tonbridge and Ashford were allowed 31 minutes, with a Schools, a Spam or even an Arthur. So I decided we would see what our Coppertop could do, knowing that Harry could keep her on the mark. By Paddock Wood we were doing 50 and she was picking up speed nicely; we were touching 70 by Marden and up to nearly 80 m.p.h. by Headcorn. We ran into Ashford in 32½ minutes exact and, true to form, Harry had kept the 'E1' on the mark all the way. The cut-off was never less than 25 per cent and the regulator had been wide open from Paddock Wood to Headcorn . . .

Just another run on the Southern in the days before steam disappeared . . .